I0510919

FINDING, BUYING, AND DEVELOPING A SOUTH TEXAS RANCH

SECOND EDITION

Jim Mullen

Finding, Buying, and Developing a South Texas Ranch

Copyright © 2016 Jim Mullen. All rights reserved. No part of this book may be reproduced or retransmitted in any form or by any means without the written permission of the publisher.

Published by Wheatmark®
1760 East River Road, Suite 145, Tucson, Arizona 85718 USA
www.wheatmark.com

ISBN: 978-1-62787-422-9 (paperback)
ISBN: 978-1-62787-423-6 (ebook)
LCCN: 2016940683

This book is dedicated to H. Irving Schweppe, James G. Teer, Thomas Linton, Wayne Hamilton, John Lupe, and J. D. Williams, men who believed in me enough to help me learn.

It is also dedicated to J. Frank Childress, Chester Scott, John Fambrough, and Johnnie Rosenauer, brokers who taught me real estate can be an honorable profession.

And to Eileen, my light from the darkness.

This book is dedicated to H. Irving Schweppe, James G. Teer, Thomas Linton, Wayne Hamilton, John Lupe, and J. D. Williams, men who believed in me enough to help me learn.

It is also dedicated to J. Frank Childress, Chester Scott, John Fambrough, and Johnnie Rosenauer, brokers who taught me real estate can be an honorable profession.

And to Eileen, my light from the darkness.

Contents

Introduction

Of all the investment possibilities, real estate has the best long-term record. Unlike stocks, bonds, or commodities, real estate has shown a steady increase in value across the board. This is because the supply of land is finite; "they ain't making it any more" being a favorite hucksters pitch.

One tiny portion of the surface of the Earth is known as Texas, a land of greatly varying weather, inhospitable flora and fauna, and home to a hardscrabble citizenry that has learned to endure and thrive. Texas is the romantic stuff of legends; legends of cowboys and Indians, cowmen and crooks, rattlesnakes and oil.

Driving a pasture road at sunrise or sundown is the best time to appreciate the romance of Texas. Mid-day it may be 110 degrees at eye level, 130 at the surface; a time when Man is the only animal dumb enough to be out. But when the sun is waxing or waning and not at full strength, and the shadows lengthen, the abundant wildlife begins to stir, either heading out to feed or heading for daytime shade and you begin to realize just how rich the habitat is. Colors that were bleached in direct sunlight become vivid and the breeze that dehydrates you at noon carries a bit of moisture and the musty smell of a fecund ecology.

I believe it is this complex living puzzle comprised of earth, climate, vegetation, and animals that draws humans to buy land in Texas. On the surface, for some it may be the desire to shoot a trophy deer, bag a limit of quail or dove, fish their own, private stocktank, or run a hobby herd of cows. Underneath, however, I believe that the romance and the belief that this land, once conquered, will produce abundantly for whoever has the gumption to take it on, is why people buy land in Texas.

In this book, I will expose the prospective ranch buyer to the basic principles of buying and developing rural land in South and Central Texas. The book may well raise more questions than answers, but at least you'll have a better idea of what questions need asking.

Section 1

LOOKING FOR YOUR RANCH

Buying a ranch is often the greatest investment a buyer will make in his or her lifetime and should not be undertaken lightly. Admittedly, while ranches are simply toys for some people, land ownership and the transfer of ownership is serious business. Unlike a car, you cannot just "take it back" if you find something doesn't suit you. Buying a ranch is a major undertaking, with a lot of aspects you may not be familiar with. You're going to need some help.

Finding a Broker

Regardless of how you find and buy your ranch, you'll probably do business with a farm and ranch Broker, one licensed by the Texas Real Estate Commission (TREC) to assist in the transfer of ownership of real estate. Yes, you can dig a hole with your hand, and you can buy a ranch by yourself, working directly with the Seller. However, just as digging is easier with a shovel, so is buying a ranch with a Broker. Most ranch buyers today are not ranchers by trade, and may not know exactly what they're buying. While they might be the greatest doctor, lawyer, or even commercial broker on the face of the earth, they often don't know the difference between guajillo and blackbrush; sandy loam and clay. A RANCH Broker should know the difference and should know what you need to be satisfied.

What then is this animal, known as a Broker? As recently as 30 years ago, ranch Brokers were a closed lot. In South Texas there were perhaps 5 "successful" Brokers, Brokers that sold across South Texas and sold more than 25,000 acres a year. These few pretty much were the extent of the farm and ranch real estate industry. In those days the laws were pretty loose and for "$10 and a letter of character recommendation", you could become a Broker in Texas.

This changed with the land bust of the early 1980's, when land in Frio Co., for example, went from $1,200 to $400 per acre. With good ranches being auctioned at local hotels and banks peddling their foreclosures to anyone with decent credit and a small down payment, a new class of buyer was introduced. Because of the glut of properties, the sharing of information and professionalism became crucial to a Broker's survival. "Hip pocket" listings, listings where the Broker knew of a place that could be bought, but no signed agreement existed between the Owner and the Broker, became rare as first time buyers became the norm rather than the exception.

This was because these first time buyers were not cattlemen but were successful business men; usually at least one generation away from the land. They were looking primarily for recreation property, not a source of income, and they were used to doing business in writing, using lawyers and expert advisors to accomplish their transactions. This professionalism dictated a change in the way Brokers did business and precipitated a change in the industry. The Texas Real Estate Commission (TREC) stepped in too, stiffening education requirements, upgrading the licensing process, and revising the forms used in rural land sales. The "good ol' boys" and their slipshod way of doing business were out.

Today, farm and ranch real estate brokerage is strictly regulated and supervised by TREC. As a group, we gradually came to accept the FAX, the mobile phone, and eventually, with much wailing and gnashing of teeth, the computer. In the last 20 years the business has undergone major changes, all to the benefit of the consumer.

Brokers are required to have two years of experience as salespersons under the tutelage of an established Broker, and must pass an additional test to become a Broker. Like many professionals today, farm and ranch Brokers, with few exceptions, must undergo mandatory continuing education every two years to renew their license. They are required to use the forms promulgated by a Lawyer-Broker Committee at TREC, and must be well versed in their duties.

Unlike residential Brokers, farm and ranch Brokers normally work alone, sometimes with one or two salespersons; salespersons doing their time before they can become Brokers. It is important to note that most farm and ranch Brokers do only farm and ranch. I fear many Buyers do not get the best property or best deal possible, because they do not seek out a farm and ranch specialist.

Broker responsibilities fall into several categories, starting with a basic two; those that represent the Seller or those that represent the Buyer. If a Broker has a listing agreement with a Seller that Broker normally represents the Seller. He is compensated by the Seller for completing the sale at a rate negotiated between the two. This compensation, called the commission, is that Brokers' money, to do with as he sees fit. He can, of course, keep it all, for a job well done. He may give some of the commission to either the Seller or the Buyer at closing, to help with closing costs, or to "make the deal". He may also give some of his commission to another Broker for that Brokers' assistance, called "splitting" the commission. The "other" Broker may assist the Listing Broker as a sub-agent, representing the Seller, or he may assist as the Buyer's representative, representing the Buyer yet still be paid by the Listing Broker. This is a major and fairly recent change. When I got in the business, we all worked for the Seller because we and had a fiduciary link to the Seller. Once the commission was deemed to belong to the Listing Broker, to do with as he sees fit, it allowed other Brokers to represent the Buyer, a major difference. In an instance where the Broker represents both parties, an "intermediary" relationship is formed. This is complex and fraught with potential problems and should be avoided.

To make this all clear, at the first substantial meeting between any Broker and prospective Buyer, the form below should be supplied to the Buyer. This form, promulgated by TREC, sets forth the duties and obligations of the Brokers in any transaction. As I often say when handing it to a Buyer, "you can't tell the players without a program." This form identifies the players and delineates their loyalties.

Information About Brokerage Services

11-2-2015

Texas law requires all real estate license holders to give the following information about brokerage services to prospective buyers, tenants, sellers and landlords.

TYPES OF REAL ESTATE LICENSE HOLDERS:
- **A BROKER** is responsible for all brokerage activities, including acts performed by sales agents sponsored by the broker.
- **A SALES AGENT** must be sponsored by a broker and works with clients on behalf of the broker.

A BROKER'S MINIMUM DUTIES REQUIRED BY LAW (A client is the person or party that the broker represents):
- Put the interests of the client above all others, including the broker's own interests;
- Inform the client of any material information about the property or transaction received by the broker;
- Answer the client's questions and present any offer to or counter-offer from the client; and
- Treat all parties to a real estate transaction honestly and fairly.

A LICENSE HOLDER CAN REPRESENT A PARTY IN A REAL ESTATE TRANSACTION:

AS AGENT FOR OWNER (SELLER/LANDLORD): The broker becomes the property owner's agent through an agreement with the owner, usually in a written listing to sell or property management agreement. An owner's agent must perform the broker's minimum duties above and must inform the owner of any material information about the property or transaction known by the agent, including information disclosed to the agent or subagent by the buyer or buyer's agent.

AS AGENT FOR BUYER/TENANT: The broker becomes the buyer/tenant's agent by agreeing to represent the buyer, usually through a written representation agreement. A buyer's agent must perform the broker's minimum duties above and must inform the buyer of any material information about the property or transaction known by the agent, including information disclosed to the agent by the seller or seller's agent.

AS AGENT FOR BOTH - INTERMEDIARY: To act as an intermediary between the parties the broker must first obtain the written agreement of *each party* to the transaction. The written agreement must state who will pay the broker and, in conspicuous bold or underlined print, set forth the broker's obligations as an intermediary. A broker who acts as an intermediary:
- Must treat all parties to the transaction impartially and fairly;
- May, with the parties' written consent, appoint a different license holder associated with the broker to each party (owner and buyer) to communicate with, provide opinions and advice to, and carry out the instructions of each party to the transaction.
- Must not, unless specifically authorized in writing to do so by the party, disclose:
  ○ that the owner will accept a price less than the written asking price;
  ○ that the buyer/tenant will pay a price greater than the price submitted in a written offer; and
  ○ any confidential information or any other information that a party specifically instructs the broker in writing not to disclose, unless required to do so by law.

AS SUBAGENT: A license holder acts as a subagent when aiding a buyer in a transaction without an agreement to represent the buyer. A subagent can assist the buyer but does not represent the buyer and must place the interests of the owner first.

TO AVOID DISPUTES, ALL AGREEMENTS BETWEEN YOU AND A BROKER SHOULD BE IN WRITING AND CLEARLY ESTABLISH:
- The broker's duties and responsibilities to you, and your obligations under the representation agreement.
- Who will pay the broker for services provided to you, when payment will be made and how the payment will be calculated.

LICENSE HOLDER CONTACT INFORMATION: This notice is being provided for information purposes. It does not create an obligation for you to use the broker's services. Please acknowledge receipt of this notice below and retain a copy for your records.

Licensed Broker/Broker Firm Name or Primary Assumed Business Name	License No.	Email	Phone
Designated Broker of Firm	License No.	Email	Phone
Licensed Supervisor of Sales Agent/ Associate	License No.	Email	Phone
Sales Agent/Associate's Name	License No.	Email	Phone

Buyer/Tenant/Seller/Landlord Initials	Date

Regulated by the Texas Real Estate Commission   Information available at www.trec.texas.gov

IABS 1-0

James M. Mullen, REALTOR, 102 CR 4773 Castroville, TX 78009   Phone: 210 260-5946   Fax: 830 538 9406   Las Tres to Prophes
James Mullen   Produced with zipForm® by zipLogix 18070 Fifteen Mile Road, Fraser, Michigan 48026   www.zipLogix.com

Unfortunately, there are "bad apples" in every business and obscurity is their haven. In addition to possibly misrepresenting information, Brokers are NOT attorneys and should not advise you on any matter regarding the law. You should not rely on him/her for advice of a legal nature. As a Buyer, you should always keep in mind that real estate professionals in Texas are subject to the TREC and there is a venue for complaints against Brokers and salespersons. Do not hesitate to complain to TREC if you feel you have been mistreated or misled by any real estate professional.

Many Buyers feel that they can best find the property they want by looking at the classifieds and visiting Listing Broker websites, then contacting the Listing Broker for a viewing. The mistake they make is that they simply do not see all that is available. Not all Brokers have websites and not all properties make it to the web. Brokers that have listings would prefer you buy their properties and may not show you other properties listed by other Brokers. Also, the Buyer may not fully understand what requirements he/she has in terms of location, soils, vegetation, etc. and may not know what questions to ask of the Listing Broker. Lastly, they may be "bullied" during the contract phase to either pay too much or give up rights they may not even know they have. This is not to say Listing Brokers are evil. Many Brokers do both, taking listings as well as representing Buyers. I do just that and in truth do not change my presentation regardless of my fiduciary responsibilities. But it is crucial, in my opinion, for a buyer, particularly a first-time Buyer to have his/her own Broker, a "buyer's rep", looking out for his/her best interests.

I should point out that there is an option for a Buyer to retain a Broker as his representative and negotiate a commission with him/her. This has been the case for several years, but has not caught on. My thought is that this is due to the relatively large commissions that have always been traditionally paid by the Sellers. The Buyers feel that they are paying one commission anyway in the purchase price and, since they're not going to get a "break" in the purchase price by paying another Broker to represent them, why should they pay a buyer representation commission? Happily, it is the norm for Listing Brokers and Buyer Rep. Brokers to work together, splitting the commission. Both parties are represented at no additional cost to the Buyer.

Be sure any Broker you work with is licensed by TREC.

Picking a good Broker to represent you early on in the purchasing process should fill in the gaps in your knowledge and experience as well as make the process go smoother. How do you go about finding a Broker to represent you, a Broker suited to your needs? First of all, you need to decide in general what type of land you are looking for, where you would prefer it be located, what you intend to do with the land, and how much you can afford. Once you've chosen a Broker, these parameters can be refined, but a rough idea of your needs is needed in choosing a Broker.

Once you have these questions pretty well answered in your mind, it is time to seek out a professional farm and ranch Broker. Please, do not ask your wife's third cousin who just got his/her real estate license to "see what's for sale". It wastes his/her time, your time, and any other Brokers' time. You need a farm and ranch Broker, one who specializes in the area you want and the type/size property you want to purchase. You should look for a member of the Texas Association of Realtors, if for no other reason than they have and adhere to a code of ethics. That alone will make the purchase process more open and above board. If possible, find a Broker that has the Accredited Buyer Representative (ABR) designation. That simply means that the Broker has attended classes designed to help him/her protect your interests in the sale.

Word of mouth is probably the best way to find a Broker to represent you. Ask friends and relatives if they have bought or sold ranches and who the Brokers involved were. Were these Brokers honest, knowledgeable, and friendly? Did they work to present your friends with a variety of properties, trying to expose them to several selections in their price range? Location of the ranches they helped buy or sell is fairly important, although farm and ranch Brokers usually cover large geographic areas. An exception would be when you want to be in a specific area or near a specific town. In that case, small town Brokers who work their counties and little outside that may suffice. They are excellent sources for information, but limited to their areas and normally sell just their own listings. I feel it is better to try to find a Broker that has experience in your preferred area, but works a broad area, just to widen the scope of your search. After all, you probably are not familiar with, *all* of South Texas or *all* of the Texas Hill Country. Once you find a Broker to represent you, let him/her go to the Brokers in that small town and see if they have any properties that you might be interested in.

Failing to find a likely candidate from among your friends, you can type "South Texas Ranches for Sale" in your search engine for a list of websites that should apply. Read the Broker bios on these websites and pick a few to call. Ask specifically if they do Buyer Representation and ask for their sales history and references. Any qualified, experienced Broker will be happy to send you his/her sales history and from that you can pick those Brokers that have sold in the area and size you're looking for.

As a last resort, check out the classifieds on the San Antonio Express-News, the Houston Chronicle, the Austin American-Statesman or the Livestock Weekly. These periodicals, while steadily shrinking, still have "Farms and Ranches For Sale" sections. Look through these ads, noting Brokers that are selling ranches in the size you need, in the areas you prefer. Call several, explaining what you are looking for and ask if they have anything that might fit your needs. Ask if they will represent you in looking at ranches listed by other Brokers. If they agree, ask for e-mail or written packages on all the ranches they are aware of that fit your requirements. The fact that you have asked for and received information on certain ranches from a Listing Broker in no way obligates you to that Broker. At any time, you can say you desire to be represented by another Broker and he/she must respect that request. He/

She may say however, that he/she does not want to share the commission, either because it is too small to be split, or because he/she feels they have earned the whole commission. At that time, you must decide if the property is interesting enough to seek out and compensate your own Broker. Also, if the Broker seems pushy or eager to go look at ranches before you feel ready, find another Broker; this is too important an investment to fall for the hard sell. Along the same lines, if you pick a Broker with listings which generally fit your requirements, the Broker will often favor his listings over those of another Broker. This reduces the scope of your search and leaves you without any representation. If at all possible, choose a Broker without any listings that fit your search parameters; let him/her represent you and see all that's out there.

During this initial phase, ask the Brokers you call about their business and their experience. Try to find one that is compatible and is eager to help you, not just sell those properties he or she has listed. If they are not willing to seek other properties, if for no other reason than to compare with their listings, they are not representing you and you will not get the best selection to choose from.

Once you have selected a Broker to represent you and search for likely properties for you, show him/her some loyalty. Once you start looking, you will start to receive calls from Brokers, offering you properties and their services. It makes life and the buying process much easier if you simply refer them to your Broker. Nothing complicates what can be a pleasurable experience more than multiple Brokers fighting over a commission. Pick a Broker and force all information through him/her. Doing this, the process will be much simpler, reducing stress and avoiding lawsuits when it comes time to close. It is very important that you visit prospective properties with the same Broker. An unwritten rule among Brokers is that, whomever showed the property to the Buyer is the procuring cause of the sale and is due compensation. If you feel you are not seeing all that there is to see in your search category, tell your Broker. If the situation does not change, you may well consider changing Brokers.

Setting Your Parameters

O.K., now you have decided on one Broker to represent you in the search for and purchase of your "dream" ranch. You have ensured that this broker has participated in the sale/purchase of similar properties in the past in the areas you prefer. I harp on experience for several reasons, one in particular. As a new salesperson, I went on my first showing alone with the buyer. We went all over this ranch, climbing into deer stands, turning on water wells, peeking into sheds and barns, a good, through, look at the property. It was not until I returned to the office and began gathering answers for the Buyer's questions that I noticed some irregularities. There were six wells, not four, and the field near the camp was no more than 30 acres, not the 125 in the brochure. Turns out I was on the wrong ranch the whole time. I had done an excellent job of showing a ranch that was not for sale. I thank my lucky stars the Buyer was not interested enough to make an offer!

Now it is time to meet or call your (experienced) Broker and set the parameters for your search. The first is of course, price. What do you want to spend on this ranch, knowing that there will be expenses after closing to develop the property? Unless you're paying cash, or doing a 1031 tax-free exchange, you should contact your sources of money to learn about interest rates and loan types to see what you're qualified for well before you start looking at ranches. Ranch loans come under a different category than either residential or commercial loans and ranch loans may be structured differently with different rates. Your local bank or credit union will probably not make a ranch loan. If it does, the rate may be higher than a financial institution that specializes in such loans. Again using the internet, typing in "farm and ranch loans" in your search engine will bring up a list of such institutions, such as Frost Bank, Crockett National Bank, Capital Farm Credit, etc.

Remember to include improvements and equipment in your loan estimates. Many a time, I've seen new ranch owners over-extend themselves, trying to make improvements on a shoestring budget; having to wait several years before they can afford to make the improvements they want. While stretching improvements out over several years is fine, at a minimum, leave enough in the kitty to allow you to enjoy the place; that's ultimately why you're buying a ranch, to enjoy, not worry.

Size of your dream ranch is a function of price and location. First of all, ranches are normally priced per acre, as opposed to the total, unless the improvements are a significant contributor to the total. This helps Brokers and Buyers compare ranches and use comparable sales as references. If you have $5,000,000.00 to spend, you have to decide if you'd rather have 3,300 acres in Kinney County, 2,000 acres in Dimmit County, or 500 acres in Kerr Co. Why the big difference, in a relatively small area? Prices vary greatly and are determined to some extent by several variables in a very imprecise, fluid manner. In South Texas, location, primarily distance from San Antonio, is perhaps the greatest variable, as Buyers from Houston, Austin, or Dallas are in for a long trip regardless. Prices decline as drive time from

S.A. increases. An exception would be the George West-Beeville area, where easy access from Houston on Hwy. 59 and Corpus on IH 37 seems to inflate prices a bit.

Another factor is wildlife potential, particularly Whitetail deer. Today's Buyer is primarily interested in deer, with brush selling much quicker, and for more money, than improved rangeland or farmland, even though farmland has a potential for income and can be easily converted to good quail hunting. Deer hunting still drives the market however, so ranch property in counties with a reputation for producing big deer sells for more. The "golden triangle" is a good example. This area, bounded by Cotulla, Laredo, and Eagle Pass has been promoted over the years as having produced superior deer. While it is true that Dimmit Co., smack in the middle of this triangle, has more listings in the Boone and Crockett book, "book" deer are becoming more prevalent throughout the region, due to high fencing, supplemental feed, and sound management. While I still get calls for properties in the "golden triangle", more buyers today are looking for sand or red sand, a soil type rather than a location. This is because of the greater vegetative response to moisture with sand and sandy loam soils and because it is harder to get stuck on opening morning in red sand than in clay. Hunters are nothing if not practical.

Soils in South Texas vary greatly, but have been well mapped by the Natural Resource Conservation Service (NRCS), formerly known as the Soil Conservation Service (SCS). On one ranch I managed for a time, I had 12 different soils on 1,600 acres, each with its' own characteristics. Start with a general soils map to narrow your search for specific soils, knowing that variations will occur.

Parts of South Texas are well known for certain soils. For example, Dilley to Carrizo Springs is red sand and Tilden to

Freer is clay loam. North of Hebbronville is a sandy-clay soil with caliche outcrops while south of town it turns to a deep sand. This ties in with vegetation; if you want guajillo, you'll want to focus on the counties with sandy, gravelly ridges. If you want blackbrush, look to those areas with more clay.

Lastly, rainfall affects price. In general, rainfall in South Texas decreases as you move westward from the Gulf of Mexico and southward from the Balconies Escarpment or Hill Country. Within this general rule, there are exceptions, as always; areas that always seem to miss the rains or get more than others. An experienced Broker can help you with this, as can talking with locals. Long-term averages are helpful, although I was told a long time ago that the 10-year average rainfall in South Texas is the result of a "hurricane followed by 9 years of drought".

So, distance from the big cities, wildlife potential, soils, and rainfall are the gross determinants of price. Water is critical to the development and enjoyment of a ranch and critical to the investment value of a ranch in today's market. Rapid changes in how we view, use, and regulate water resources make water a very important consideration in buying a ranch. We'll talk more about water as it relates to development, but it should not limit your search area unless you intend to use it for irrigation. As always, there are exceptions to this rule too. Some areas of South Texas do not have well water, at least not at depths that are economically feasible. I once sold a place SW of Tilden, an area known for very deep well water. Those new owners had to re-enter a plugged oil well, drilling out five concrete plugs to finally reach water at 4,800 feet. Even with that, the water produced is hot and full of mineral once it finally reaches the surface. Situations such as this certainly affect the utility of the land and ultimately the price.

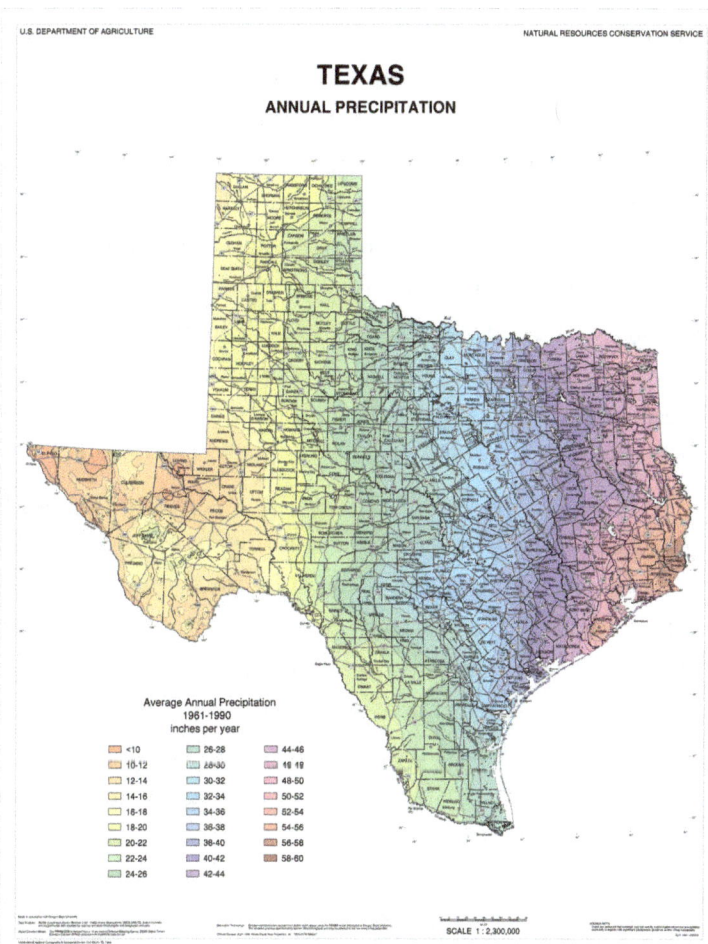

Moisture drives the machine in Texas; always consider rainfall.

Politics and social considerations may well figure into the choice of location as well. Some areas have reputations for trespass, poaching and/or burglary, and operating a ranch in these areas, while not prohibitive, requires additional thought regarding safety and security

Remember too, this doesn't have to be your only or "last" ranch. If new to the experience, buy a smaller place, fix it up, and trade it in for a bigger one several years down the road. I know quite a few people who do this and sometimes make good money at it. Just don't expect to get rich at flipping ranches unless you have the capital and the time to get good at it.

Improvements are a personal matter. I've heard several times over the years that a Buyer would take the ranch offered if it did not have the improvements in place. If the house does not match the idea of what you (or your wife) want, it probably won't work. The house aside, look for basic improvements done well; water, fencing, outbuildings, fields, roads, etc. These are generic improvements that cost a lot in both time and money but usually are not reflected in the price. Unless you plan to buy a ranch big enough to justify a caretaker or manager, making improvements can be a frustrating, drawn out process. Arranging for, then meeting with contractors at the ranch can require several trips a week. Buying a place with a barn or water well already in place saves you a lot of hassle. And just for grins, taste the well water, you may be surprised!

Speaking of traveling to the ranch, access is usually near the top of most Buyers' wish lists. Paved frontage, while increasing the chances of trespass, does ensure that you can get to, and home from the ranch. Preferred access options include paved access on a dead end road, so poachers and burglars feel "trapped" on that road, but the landowner can still get in and out easily. Conversely, some buyers want isolation and prefer to be at the very end of the road or at the end of an easement. This works if you plan to stay at the ranch for extended periods of time or have the money to weather-proof the entry road. Always remember that, even in deep South Texas, there are occasions, usually during deer season, when dirt roads may become impassable and four-wheel-drive trucks are nothing more than very comfortable, stationary deer blinds. Four days before writing this, I was stuck in La Salle Co. in a new 4WD pickup, extended cab with all the bells and whistles. It was so stuck, in red SAND, that a jeep could not move us, another truck could not budge us and it was not until a road grader arrived four hours later that we were pulled from that damn hole. While I freely admit the sunset was beautiful, it was not nearly as beautiful as that old motor grader coming over the rise.

Lastly, minerals, or the lack thereof, should be a consideration when deciding on your search parameters. Because minerals, and now water rights, are such an important part of the value of rural property, particularly in South Texas, this is one area that should be thoroughly explored in the early stages. Whether or not you receive any mineral interest at all, whether or not there is, or could be, any mineral activity in your area, and whether or not you could live with drilling, pumping, hauling, etc. are all very important considerations. Do not go to the contract stage simply asking for "all owned minerals". Find out what minerals are owned and what percentage will be conveyed. This is a key negotiating point in the purchase and you should know going in what you're getting and what you require to be satisfied. If the ranch has not changed hands for many years, the owner may not know what mineral rights he/ she owns. This is rare with today's "oil boom" in Texas, but it still may happen. If you feel you must have some mineral rights to be comfortable with a purchase, say so early on and make it a condition of the purchase. Be cautious of a prospectus that says "minerals to be determined by title search". This may well mean there are no minerals to convey and the just want to get you on paper hoping you'll learn to live with a surface-only (no mineral rights) ranch.

First of all, let me say that as a Broker, I refer all mineral questions to an attorney. Minerals in Texas are separate from the surface and a precise understanding is necessary. I often hear from Buyers that they want 50% of the minerals so they will be "in control" of any mineral development. It is just not that simple. I believe I am safe in saying that mineral rights in South Texas are usually marketed in three forms; mineral rights, executive rights, and royalty rights. This is a dangerous generalization as the mineral estate can be divided into more than three simple parts. In yet another informative publication; "Rights and Responsibilities of Mineral Cotenants", Judon Fambrough, a down to earth attorney for The Real Estate Center at Texas A&M University states: "The mineral estate comprises five separate and distinct interests: (1) the right to lease the mineral property, sometimes called the *executive right*; (2) the right to develop and produce the minerals; (3) the right to receive bonuses; (4) the right to receive delay rentals; and (5) the right to receive royalties." These five rights may still be all in one bundle, but they may be separated out and available to you, the Buyer in varying percentages or not at all. Suffice it to say, this is an important aspect of buying land in South Texas. Basic information on minerals, and a wealth of other subjects concerning rural land, is available from The Real Estate Center at A&M (http://recenter.tamu.edu/). Certainly if there is ever any question, ask an attorney, preferably one experienced in oil and gas law before you commit.

I recently negotiated a sale where the Sellers did not know what mineral interests they had. They thought they owned all the minerals and were offering half of all *owned* minerals. To avoid surprises, my buyer wrote in that he would receive *50% of 100% of the mineral estate*, or the deal was off. This choice of words eliminated the chance of an "oops!" at closing, where the Seller finds out he/she really did not own any minerals yet the Buyer is already thinking what color to paint the barn. It's in awkward situations such as this that everybody calls their lawyers. Such situations should never occur. If a Seller is unsure of what portion of the mineral estate they own, it should be researched even before the asking price is set. True, some of it will come out in the title search, but minerals are not generally well defined by the title commitment and are not guaranteed by the title policy. A plus of the current oil boom is that landmen, people that research mineral rights, are plentiful and a mineral search is fairly inexpensive. A mineral search can usually be done in two weeks, and is a good expenditure during the Option Period (see contracts following).

Sometimes the Seller does not own any minerals or simply does not want to convey any. That is not to say the property is worthless to you as a buyer. As the new owner, you will still own the surface, and have some say in what goes on. You can still manage the deer, plant crops, dig stocktanks, you just may have some new "neighbors" move in and bring their drilling rig with them. It is important to know that the mineral estate is dominant to the surface estate. In Texas, if they have a right to recover minerals from under your land, they can do pretty much anything reasonable without your consent. If you can live with that, and many do with no problem, then you can get good ranch property at a reduced cost.

I hear from a lot of Buyers that oil production equates to poor deer since all the trophy deer are shot by the roughnecks or by the gaugers. While this may have been true at one time, and while I do not doubt that it occasionally happens today, most oil field workers have no interest in shooting your deer. For one thing, they would have to conceal the carcass in their vehicle to get it off the property, blood, guts, and all, exposing themselves while loading it and having to remove all signs of blood. For another, they would have to carry a rifle with them, against the rules on an oil lease, and hope no one hears the shot. Violation of the restriction against hunting or carrying a firearm is grounds for dismissal so, unless the worker doesn't need his job, or the whole crew is in on it, it's just not going to happen.

I am often asked what is the minimum number of acres needed to produce quality deer or quail in huntable numbers? There is no "minimum" as long as the animals can pass freely across your boundaries. Of course, depending on the species, this means that under a certain size, you will be "sharing" wildlife with your neighbors. High fencing addresses this issue for most mammals, by enclosing wild populations inside a net wire fence that restricts movement. With a high fence, you can manage a pen of less than 1 acre for trophy deer; is that then the minimum? Bobwhite quail normally distribute themselves over suitable habitat for nesting at a density of one pair for every 4 acres. Is that the minimum? Of course not. If you want to manage a self-sustaining, free-ranging population, but your financial situation limits your ranch to a modest size, study your potential neighbors carefully. A smaller size tract does not necessarily mean you cannot have an enjoyable experience as a landowner; it just means that the smaller tracts require more management planning and may involve cooperation with your neighbors.

The Prospectus

The prospectus, or "package", is a valuable tool in looking for a ranch. When I started in the business back in the 80's, packages were paper and consisted of a text description of the ranch, some deer pics, a location map, and a topo. Now, with advances in technology, a "package" can include video, both on the ground and from a drone, enhanced color pictures, and various links to additional information. Content varies a lot between brokers and the larger companies have of course larger budgets for promotional materials. What I used to put in the mail to clients is now available online at the touch of a mouse multiplied a hundred fold.

Because of this new technology, well before you get in the car to take a look, you should have a pretty good idea of what is being offered for sale. The prospectus should be more that pretty pictures of big deer, more than exhortations of urgency to sell, and certainly more than a drone tour of the Brush Country. In my opinion the prospectus, written or online, should include, at a minimum, the following items:

Location

This paragraph should include, among other things, distance

365 acres in Medina County

Quailpro LLc | 210-260-4946 | quailpro@sbcglobal.net

Property Address

Quihi, Texas 78861

Property Highlights
- Price: $1,733,750.00
- Acres: 365.00
- County: Medina
- State: Texas
- Closest City: Quihi
- Property Type: Acreage

Property Description

Description: The Matthews Ranch is an excellent farm/ranch combination with good soils, superior water, and good fencing. Approximately 300 acres are cleared and in either dryland or irrigated farmland. The balance is cleared with light regrowth and heavy grass; suitable for quail hunting with some deer/hog hunting.

Location/Topography: The ranch is located on FM 2676, some 7 miles west of Rio Medina or 5 miles NE of Quihi.

Water: In addition to Quihi Creek, the ranch has an Edwards irrigation well, equipped with an immaculate diesel engine. This water is piped to two pivot points, a side-roll point, and the pond.

Improvements: In addition to the Edwards well, windmill, and pivots, the ranch has an extensive fence system suitable for high-intensity cattle rotation, two fair to poor sets of working pens, and some sheds in marginal condition.

Wildlife: Dove hunting is superior on this property, even if the farming is not done here. As mentioned, there is suitable quail habitat on the east side, and I can personally attest to the numbers of deer that can be lured onto the ranch.

Minerals: Sellers believe they own 50% of the mineral estate and 100% of the Executive Rights. There is no production and the amount to be conveyed is negotiable.

Jim Mullen
quailpro@sbcglobal.net
210-260-4946
102 CR 4773
Castroville, TX 78009
www.quailpro.com
More details at landsoftexas.com/listing/2982969

Driving Directions
Midway between Rio Medina and Quihi on the east side of FM 2676

Get all the info you can before you get in the car.

from towns, type of access to the ranch (paved, deeded easement, recorded easement), size of neighbors and their management history. This information can be gleaned from maps and the Seller. Normally the Buyer does NOT contact neighbors as the offering may not be public knowledge. Alerting the neighbors, (and any ranch staff), that the ranch is for sale may aggravate the Seller and taint the transaction. Be cautious, on the other hand, of a Seller that specifically demands you not contact the neighbors. There may well be something suspicious about that.

Description

This is the meat of the package and should fully describe the soils, vegetation, topography, and dimensions of the ranch. This paragraph tells you what you are really buying as these factors determine to a large extent what you will be able to do with the ranch. Normally mentioned here is the management history of the place with regards to brush. Where brush has been cleared or treated, how it was treated, and when. What fields there are on the ranch and what they have been used for in the past. It is also nice to know what changes there are in elevation across the ranch to give you a feel of the place.

A lot of ink goes into the presence of "good deer brush". While brush is a component of a deer's diet, and some amount of brush is necessary for most types of wildlife, 2,500 acres of solid guajillo is not necessarily a better deer property than one with 1,500 acres of guajillo and 1,000 acres of old field. Certainly, learn the important deer browse plants (brush), but remember that a variety of brush is very important and that forbs (weeds) and grass also contribute to a deer's annual diet. Learn to look for diversity in the brush and a good cover of vegetation on the ground. A few species of woody plants on bare ground is a sign of a problem that may require time and expensive recovery treatments such as root-plowing to correct. It may also indicate poor or saline soils.

Water

The catalyst that makes things happen in Texas is water and the single most important factor in considering a ranch if your intent is to manage for either wildlife or cattle should be a dependable source of water. In the prospectus, this should be addressed fully. Subsurface water sources, or aquifers are becoming more and more regulated in South Texas and you should be aware of limitations as well as potential production of any aquifer under your ranch. Existing wells should be described as to age, depth, equipment, production, historic use, and any distribution systems. Descriptions of large volume wells should also include pumping allowances and limitations, if any.

I have often thought that surface water is the single most important factor in the sale of a ranch. A ranch can be located 40 miles back in there by bad road, grazed off like a Wal-Mart parking lot, with a 1962 trailer for a camp house, and still bring good money if it has several big lakes. It is just part of the romance I mentioned in that a big lake is proof of Man over Nature, a victory over the heat and desolation.

A word of caution here; on the last ranch I managed, I was initially hired to develop the new acquisition. One of the features of the new ranch was a large lake, perhaps 20 acres when full. The Broker, who shall remain nameless, assured the buyer, my new boss, that the lake had great fishing and was probably 10 feet deep at the dam. While one of the sales pitches was watching fish swirl out in the lake, perhaps it would have been good to note that the fish swirling were carp and gar and the "lake" was only 18 inches deep at its' deepest point! It was not until years later that a severe drought allowed us to clean that tank at a considerable expense and restore it to productivity. Be careful of information given as part of a sale. For the most part, information is probably true, but if they claim a tank is 10 feet deep, then they can, and should prove it with a line, sinker, and cork.

Rivers are a separate concern and it should be clearly stated where the property line is and what riparian rights, if any, you will receive. In some instances, ranches that adjoin along a river swap sides; fencing down to the water part of the way, then back off the river for the rest, so ranches across from each other have access to water cows without mingling the herd. This, however, is based on an agreement and usually does not change the true property lines. Some rivers can be drawn from for domestic and livestock use, others are fully restricted, like the Nueces River, which belongs wholly to Corpus Christi.

Lastly, average rainfall should be part of the prospectus. If not, data on average rainfall is readily available for most South Texas towns and you can extrapolate rainfall on your ranch from that. As discussed, though, "average rainfall" is a joke and you should always look to the vegetation and stocktanks to get a true idea of the frequency and volume of rainfall in the area of the ranch under consideration. Simply looking at the vegetation on native range in Brackettville and comparing that to that on similar soils in Three Rivers is an example of what I mean.

Improvements

In the prospectus, all improvements that contribute to the price should be described. Buildings, fences (boundary and interior), roads, pens, deer blinds and feeders, if included in the sale, and water systems should all be described. Admittedly, these things do not normally constitute a significant portion of the purchase price, but they do contribute to the overall picture of the property that you build in your head. If the ranch has a house, it is important to know before the decision is made to take a look at the property if the house is a two room shack without power or a 3/2 brick with screened porches all around. Pictures are nice, but may be misleading. If a preview by your Broker is possible, where he and the listing Broker tour the ranch, it can be valuable to flesh out your idea of the improvements and help you decide whether or not to include a ranch in your list of "possibles".

Improvements on a ranch can be a double-edged sword. On one hand, having improvements in place means you won't have to make the expenditures to put them in. On the other hand, if they are extensive, or don't exactly fit your plans, you may have maintenance costs that you really don't need. Consider the improvements carefully when reviewing the prospectus.

Management

Past management is important to know as it will determine the productivity of your new ranch for several years, perhaps many years, yet is rarely mentioned in the prospectus other than to say "trophy management in place" or "managed for superior fishing". Except for deer harvest records, few Sellers offer any insight into what has been done to a particular tract of land without prodding. Obviously, turning a row crop operation into a deer ranch will be difficult and take a long time, while turning that same farm into a bird operation may take only two years and turning it into an intensive cattle operation may not take any time at all. Try to learn what it was used for in the past three years, then the past 20 years. If used for grazing, ask how many cows and what grazing system was used. If "managed" for hunting, ask for a copy of harvest records and pictures. One ranch I sold near Pearsall happened to also be a wildlife client of mine and I was able to provide five years worth of management plans and records to prospective Buyers. That was helpful, but more importantly, it was a critical part of the purchase price as we had said it was "managed". If it has been managed, ask for proof other than a few pictures.

Intensive farming in the past often involved the use of chemicals which, while legal and widely accepted then, are banned now. If there was any intensive farming on a prospective property, or herbicide treatment of brush before 1990, that should be disclosed so you can plan on a Phase 1 environmental assessment as part of your offer. I recently sold an old melon farm in La Salle Co. and I toured the ranch with an environmental inspector. Rather than look around the property, he spent the day in the trash dump and poking into the old barns and sheds. I asked him what he was looking for and he replied that if there were any contaminating chemicals used on the place, unless long buried, there would be drums in the sheds or dumps. That inspection, coupled with a review of aerials to find dead spots, and a review of oil lease activity in the courthouse, pretty much constituted that Phase 1.

In another instance, I was representing the buyer and we noticed a large black spot near the barn. Now, cleaning up is part of getting a place ready to sell, so I asked the Seller if that was an old set of pens or a shed he had burned. "No" he replied, "that's where I pile old batteries and set them on fire to recover the lead". Needless to say, that whole area had to be excavated prior to closing.

Minerals

Usually, most ranch packages do a fair job of describing what mineral interests are being offered in the sale. At this stage, it is important for you to know what percentage is being offered, what percentage is owned by the Seller, if there is currently any production on the ranch, and/or if the ranch is currently leased. Beware of packages that state that the "mineral interests to be conveyed to be determined by title search". That usually means that either the Seller has very little mineral interest or that the ranch is in an area of little mineral activity. The phrase may, however, be used to gloss over the fact that you will not be receiving any minerals and the Seller does not want to stigmatize his property. Again, know what is offered before you take a look.

Price

This is normally the shortest paragraph in the package. Here should be stated the asking price, terms, if any, and if there is a willingness to split the property. The last item, a willingness to split, is perhaps more important to the Seller than the Buyer as a Buyer will not initially consider a property if it is too large. Sellers willing to sell their properties in parcels should make that fact known to encourage a greater number of prospective Buyers.

The asking price has always been a problem for me. I have often wished it were more like shopping in Sears, where the price is clearly marked and that is that. Unfortunately, in real estate, we use an "asking" to start the bidding, often inflated simply to start the bidding higher than the desired sales price. This practice scares off many qualified Buyers and limits the field. I do not see it changing, but suggest that you consider properties above your price limit and inquire as to the flexibility in the asking. If the asking is really inflated, particularly if the property has been on the market long enough to "weather" a bit, they'll say there is a lot of room in the price. I'll address negotiations later, but for now, know that the "asking" is never the "taking".

Maps

I love maps and have learned that a lot can be gleaned from a good map about a property. When I started out in this business, Frank Childress, my sponsoring Broker, kept a line of kitchen trash cans in a spare room filled with topographic maps from the USGS. When he would take a listing, or get a package from another Broker, he would go into these maps, pull out the map, (or maps), and photocopy the ranch off the maps. He probably had several thousand dollars invested in those maps and invariably a ranch would be on at least two, sometimes three individual sheets. Today, all the topographic maps are available on CD, online, or loaded on I pads, with aerials to match with great resolution. Rather than tape, cut, and copy, we can simply locate the ranch online, draw the outline, measure it as needed, and print a map out in color. Following that, we can download the aerial, boundaries already in place, and print that, too. We can mark tanks, fences, roads, fields, buildings, wells, etc. so you get a better picture. There is no reason a prospectus should not have excellent maps and aerials of the property.

The prospectus should also include a soils map. Again, what is it you're buying? The dirt. Soils maps are available online through the USDA Web Soil Survey (WSS). This is an amazing website with hundreds of pages of information available with a click. Again, zoom in on the aerial of the ranch you're researching, draw the perimeter, and start clicking on soil types, characteristics, and limitations. They are also available in the County Soils Book, published by the Dept. of Agriculture for all counties in South and Central Texas. I'll get more into soils later on, but my point here is that the information is available and should be in every prospectus.

Pictures

Okay, everybody likes to look at pictures and every prospectus should have them. Remember, though, that the pictures are taken with a sale in mind and are thus framed for best advantage. A good prospectus will show buildings, wells, fences and pens as well as a selection of surface water and brush/fields. In the late '80's and early '90's, a wave of video cameras took over the ranch real estate industry. Everybody had a stack of videos of their listings and other peoples' listings. We learned, however, that this was counter-productive. Buyers were not as eager to look at properties if they had seen the video, and no one was buying a ranch simply because of a well-made movie. Today, the rage is drone photography. A drone tour is a useful tool early in the process of considering a property. Of course, if this is not available, I can preview several ranches a day, taking pictures with the BUYER in mind, and e-mail them to him/her that evening.

Speaking of previewing, if the listing Broker does not provide you with a package containing the above information, or if you have a large selection, ask your Broker to go take a look or "preview" the ranches. This cuts down on the number of ranches you will look at personally. As a preview takes much less time than a showing, and if the ranch meets your basic search criteria, your Broker should have no problem going for a preview, nor should the listing Broker have any heartburn previewing it. Avoid looking at or even previewing everything vaguely fitting your criteria. It confuses you, frustrates your Broker, and labels you as a "looker". Once labeled as such, other Brokers will not be as cooperative, thinking you may never buy and are a waste of their time. Some Brokers are more particular than others, but all value their time to some degree and can be very selective about who they show their properties to. Yeah, yeah, they work for the Seller, and are obligated to make their best efforts at presenting the property to all prospects, but if you have a reputation as a looker, they may well drag their feet and be uncooperative.

This is the importance of a decent prospectus, either on paper or online. It allows you, the Buyer, to evaluate a property without having to go on a showing and actually looking at it, saving everyone time and effort. Get the prospectus or see it online for every ranch that sounds interesting. If you feel it is incomplete, have your Broker get everything mentioned above to "fill it out", then study it, asking questions of the listing Broker as they come to mind. Listing Brokers are a wealth of information and are usually anxious to talk about their listings. It is a far, far better thing to eliminate a property over the phone than to drive all over it and then decide you are not interested. The very worst are those Buyers that say the property is not suitable after only five minutes of a showing. They should have known before they got to the gate whether or not it had possibilities. A good prospectus will prevent wasted showing time.

A final word of caution here; in a "hot" market, you will not have time to dawdle. Assuming you are ready to start the search process, collect and evaluate the written info in a timely fashion. To avoid the "looker" label, narrow your search as quickly as possible, I find a spreadsheet helps, then schedule either a preview by your broker or a showing for yourself.

Choosing Your Ranch

Once you and your Broker have found several ranches that seem to fit your requirements, it is time to take a look, a "showing". A showing is when you finally get to take a tour of the property. Usually on the first showing, both the Listing Broker and the Buyer's Broker will be present. Follow-up showings may, at the Listing Broker's discretion, be limited to just the Buyer and his Broker. Follow-up showings are a good time to bring wives and friends, to get another perspective and to help you remember details. Children are not really a good idea as spending the day cramped in a truck, nice as they are today, looking at brush can make them cranky.

As the first showing will normally include the listing Broker, use this opportunity to ask a lot of questions. The listing Broker is your primary source for information on historic use of the ranch, neighbors, weather, and the Seller's reasons for selling. Feel free to inquire as to the asking price and minerals. How was the asking price determined? Are there any comparable sales in the area? Is there any room for negotiation in the price? Does the Seller own more of the minerals than are being offered? Who owns mineral interests outstanding in third parties? Is there any production in the area and has there been any new activity recently? If there is currently production on the ranch or on a neighboring ranch, who is the producer? An important question, usually overlooked or just assumed, is the ranch currently under an agricultural valuation for ad valorem taxes? Sometimes incorrectly called an "agricultural exemption", an agricultural valuation for farming, livestock, or wildlife is very important to your tax rate. Virtually all ranches currently have Ag valuation, but you should make sure. It does not affect your use of the place, unless it is under Ag valuation for wildlife management, in which case there is a management plan you will initially be obligated to follow.

Try to go during the week if at all possible, as even Brokers have families. Weekend showings are common, and to be expected. However, they add stress on the Brokers and increase the potential of a confrontation with the Seller. Sellers, by and large, are helpful; after all, they want to sell their ranch. However, they usually have some "sweat equity" in the land or give it some sentimental value. For this reason, they cannot be as objective as you, the Buyer, should be. They may take offense at certain critical questions if posed by the Buyer in a face to face meeting. Confrontations should be avoided; that's what Brokers are for.

Allow plenty of time to see the ranch during a showing. Initially, assuming your choices are fairly close to each other, you can see several in a day, hitting the high points. On the first showing, try to see the surface water, the improvements, and a representative sampling of the vegetation. At this time, you are just trying to eliminate possible ranches, paring the selection down to two or three. Assuming a ranch fits your pocketbook, does it feel right? Does it give you a feeling of good value? Does the ranch appear to have been abused? Can it be restored economically, assuming you have the time and

First showings should just hit the high points; water, improvements, etc.

money to restore it? How about driving distance from your home; a lot of Buyers buy a ranch only to get tired of the drive after the first year. There is nothing more annoying on Sunday afternoon than looking at a 4 hour drive with three dirty, cranky kids and two dead deer that have to be turned in to the processing plant.

After this first look, it is extremely important to provide your Broker with feedback; what you liked and disliked about each property. Which ones you would like to see in detail and what information he needs to get for you before your return trip.

On a follow-up showing, since the selection should have been pared down, take more time to explore each property, maybe one ranch in the morning and one in the afternoon. On this showing, try to travel all the roads and the perimeter if at all possible. I sold a place out of Big Wells once that really only had one oilfield road on the whole 1,700 acres. Old roads were so overgrown that you could not get a truck down them and I tore off a rearview mirror trying to do so. I finally sold it using a rented helicopter that allowed the buyer to get some idea of just what was for sale. Speaking of helicopters, I recommend anyone buying more than 200 acres spend the $800 or so to see the land from the air. On a typical brush country ranch, I estimate you can see only about 10% of the place from a car. Using a helicopter gives you a much better idea of the density and composition of the vegetation on the ranch as well as a snapshot of some of the wildlife. It will also help orient you, making later exploration of the ranch easier. It could be argued that drones make this unnecessary. I maintain that, unless the drone is under your control, it will not look everywhere equally and may well give a slanted picture of the ranch.

Study surface water impoundments, stocktanks, carefully. I carry a collapsible fishing pole with a sinker and cork to test depth on tanks. Even deep tanks can be murky because of the soil type or because of turtles, trash fish, or alligators, so clarity is not a solid indication of depth. Aquatic vegetation in summertime is a good indicator of a tanks' longevity, even though it may die back each winter, since it indicates some holding capacity. Look at the surrounding vegetation, which shows the high water mark as well as flood debris, an indicator of the watershed for the tank. Walk the edge of the water, looking for animal tracks. Nothing scientific here, but tracks will give you some idea of the relative abundance of wildlife. If you walk a tank in July and do not see any tracks, either there is another water source very close by, or there may be a shortage of wildlife in that area.

Lastly, inspect the dam. In South Texas, this is normally a misnomer in that what we see above the surface is really a dump of surplus soil. The true "dam" is the core of clay that was first "borrowed" from the pit and packed into a trench immediately under the dam. This clay-filled trench is tied into clay substrata and stops the flow of water downstream. Simply digging a hole, unless done in pure clay, will not make a dependable tank; the water may follow a subsurface stratum of sand or gravel and drain away. On an older tank, trees on the backside of the dump can compromise the dam with roots seeking water. The roots penetrate the core and pass through, precipitating a leak. Looking on the backside of the dam may show whether or not the dam has been compromised by trees. A properly-constructed, properly-maintained dam will not have significant standing water on the backside nor will it have large, lush vegetation.

Certainly, in any dam, there will be seepage; some stock-tanks losing several feet of water a year, with water going around the core and outward. Additionally, evaporation in South Texas can exceed 70 inches a year, so even well-built tanks will dry up over time making the watershed very important as that determines an impoundments' potential to capture runoff. You should at this point, have a topographic or "topo" map of the ranch. These maps are invaluable for determining the optimum location for a new tank as well as the potential of an existing one. A very rough relationship of watershed to surface acres is 100 acres of watershed should produce runoff adequate for 1 surface acre of stocktank. Certainly, vegetation, topography, and soils greatly affect runoff, just as depth of the pit on the stocktank will affect its' longevity, but this will give you some idea. Simply draw a line from the dam uphill and upstream, connecting the highpoints and circling back to the dam. The land within this circle drains to that tank.

Look at water wells, sampling the water by tasting it and taking a sample for testing at a local lab, testing not only for fecal coliform but for salts as well. Most shallow water wells in South Texas produce water with some salts yet are fine for most uses. Past a certain degree of salinity however, the water, while suitable for drinking by humans as well as wildlife, cannot be used for irrigation. Repeated use of salty water for irrigation will eventually deaden the soil due to salt accumulation. Irrigation may not be in your plans, but irrigation is an option that salty water will eliminate. Regardless, you should be aware of water quality.

If the well is equipped, run it for some time, several hours if possible, to see if it continues to produce water or does it "draw down". Sometimes electric pumps are put on a well that cannot keep up, due to a slow recharge of the underground reservoir. The well may still be perfectly suitable for a windmill or a solar pump, it is just limited.

If the well has a distribution system, be sure to ask for a map and try to find all the end points of the system. I am working on a ranch now that has a leak somewhere in a distribution system. The leak will drain a 1,550 gallon storage tank in a few days, so it is a fairly large leak. We have been unable to find the leak, even in the middle of summer, and think it may be some distance from the well. Everyone that might know where the system goes is long gone, so we may be forced to replace the whole system.

Sometimes in South Texas, the listing Broker will show you an open area with a pipe sticking up out in the middle. This is usually promoted as a "potential Carrizo well". Be cautious about these wells as there are a lot of pitfalls awaiting the Buyer. Ask if the well has been officially turned over to the Seller or is it just abandoned. Is it in fact even abandoned? If the bore has not been properly turned over to the landowner, you, as the new owner, may be liable for plugging the well even though you have no use for it and never were involved with it prior to your purchase. If the well has been signed over to the landowner, (the Seller), has it been plugged? Is the plug below the best aquifer or a shallower aquifer and, if so, may you get a copy of the plugging report? Has the well been perforated? If so, ask for the perforation records. All very important things to know about that pipe sticking up out in the pasture.

Next, with your soils map in hand, study the vegetation. On your first showing, you don't need to learn to identify those plant species important to you. At this point, it is just important to look for diversity in the vegetation. You do not want a monoculture of any one plant, no matter how good it may be. This is because the desirability or palatability of plants changes over time, so what may be the best deer browse in April is inedible in August. Likewise, while mesquite does produce a fine seed, readily eaten by a variety of animals, those seeds are only available for two weeks a year, and some years the seed production drops off to nothing. If you have a ranch with nothing but mesquite, 50 weeks of the year you're going to be out of food! No, you need diversity and by that I mean more than two types of brush and a solid turf of bufflegrass.

An important skill when assessing land in South Texas is being able to spot areas that have been disturbed by Man. In most cases, old root plowed areas will revegetate in mesquite and Twisted acacia and usually have a lot of bare ground. This is because mesquite and Twisted acacia are better competitors than other brush species. It may have a lot of bare ground initially because these two brush species draw a lot of their moisture from the surface, precluding grass and weeds from becoming established. Seeing an area with primarily mesquite and twisted acacia or huisache should indicate to you an area that is currently of lower productivity. This may be a good thing, as these areas were originally chosen as improved pasture because of more productive soils. They may be recovered as fields economically if the brush is not too large. But if you don't want a field there, or it is a large tract, remember it will be some time before that land returns to the productivity of adjoining, diverse brush land. Another trick is to spot areas that were chained or simply pushed with a bulldozer. In these areas, the mesquite trees will have multiple trunks arising from a single base. This is because removal of the top portion of a mesquite plant causes it to resprout with multiple stems. Spotting old chained or "stacked" areas is important as these areas may also have lower productivity even though diversity may not appear affected. A lot of Buyers are keyed to "virgin" mesquite. While you can still find stands of mesquite that has never been disturbed, multiple trunks, even on a big mesquite, is a strong indicator that the land has been disturbed in the distant past and those are NOT "virgin" mesquite trees.

Diversity in ground cover is important as well. Remember in the example of an old recovering root-plowed area, I mentioned that it would be brush and bufflegrass? Bufflegrass is an introduced grass that is very drought tolerant and very invasive. This is great for a cowman, but not as great for someone wanting to manage for quail or even for deer. As with brush, diversity is important in ground vegetation. Any dominance by a grass will reduce the amount of forbs on the ranch. Wildlife feed heavily on forbs (weeds), and cannot live on grass like cows. On the first showing and any subsequent showings, look for diversity in the vegetation. Ideal habitat for game species in South Texas, while varying somewhat between species, will consist of a variety of short brush with a scattering of taller trees and fairly solid groundcover consisting of weeds mixed with a variety of native bunchgrasses. The ideal may not be available, but it is important to know what to look for.

During the first showing, it is important to look at the

improvements with a critical eye. Repairing existing structures can be more expensive and time consuming than building new ones in rural areas simply because there is a shortage of quality remodel craftsmen. That old frame house that was certainly charming in 1940 may cost twice as much to remodel as a new doublewide with all the bells and whistles. Considerations at this point include power, the most important as installing power can be very expensive, water, and location of the improvements. People seem to want to put their camp or headquarters in the center of their ranch. This is not the best location, in my opinion, for several reasons. First of all, you have to improve the road from the gate to the headquarters as you will want to get in and out in all kinds of weather. Secondly, putting the headquarters in the middle of the ranch introduces noise and smells to the center, driving wildlife to the edges. Lastly, putting the improvements in the middle hides them from the public. While that may be your objective, it also increases the chances of vandalism and theft in a camp that is not occupied most of the time. Since no one can see the camp, thieves feel safer taking their time going through your stuff and loading it up, or tearing it up, at their leisure. If you have the option of locating the headquarters, put it closer to the entry, not necessarily on the road, but close enough for some ease of access and some security. If the headquarters is in place and fairly extensive, it may well have to stay. In that case, look for structural soundness and utility. There is an old saying, "you can't have too big a barn" and, while it may be true that you can never have too big a barn, you *can* have too big a house or too many houses on a ranch.

What buildings do you need on a ranch? Basically, on a working ranch, you need a house for the owner, a guest house, and houses for employees, if any. On my first ranch as manager,

I had a house, the owner had his house, and we had a smaller house for my helper, this on 5,400 acres. At the time, we had other employees, but they commuted from town. The ranch "staff" consisted of me and two or three full-time helpers. We contracted out brush work and of course called in several more helpers when we worked cows. On a recreation ranch, you may need that many houses, or you may not need more than one, your house. The need for habitations varies with size of the ranch, intensity of management, and how much of the work can be contracted out. Even filling feeders is often contracted out now, as many people do not want the hassle of full or part-time employees on their ranch. So give this some thought before you buy a place with four houses and a bunk house that sleeps 10.

Barns and outbuildings are another matter. Since these buildings ordinarily are not heated and may not even be entirely enclosed, having an extra shed or barn is not a bad deal. Maintenance on a barn is nothing compared to a house, and the openness of a barn lends it to conversion to other uses. I recently saw an old metal building south of Cotulla that had been converted into the game cleaning room. They had poured a concrete floor, using the walls as forms, added a drain, and wired it extensively for lights and outlets. They then added a door to the outside, which allowed them to hang the deer at the truck, and then bring it in out of the weather for cleaning. Completing the redo was a game cooler in the corner of the barn. For barns and outbuildings, concern yourself with the roof. If the roof is sound, that building should be O.K. without extensive maintenance, whether you plan to use it right away or not.

A lot of people ignore one of the most expensive improvements on a ranch and end up paying for it later. Fencing runs as much as $3.00 per foot for five strand barbed wire, $5.00 per foot for high fencing. Try to drive all of the perimeter fencing and where inaccessible by vehicle, get out and walk it. If it is in bad repair, know that repair or replacement costs are in your future, even if you have no intention of high fencing your ranch.

Lastly, while not an improvement; ask to see the ranch dump. This is usually in an out of the way location and may or may not need any attention. But a minimum you may want to consider having it looked at by an environmental inspector in the Phase I.

Making the Deal

After an exhaustive search, you've found a ranch that is located in the area you want, priced no more than 20% above your purchase limit, and has the soils, vegetation, and improvements that you desire. More importantly, you "like" this ranch. It is time to buy the place and get on with enjoying it.

The Farm and Ranch Contract is 9 pages of important information and conditions critical to the smooth transition of ownership of a ranch. As it changes on a regular basis, I will not reproduce it here, but trust that you have a Broker representing you that will point out the important issues as they arise. Again, your Broker is NOT an attorney, and as this is a legal document, you should have it reviewed by an attorney BEFORE you submit your first offer.

The Purchase Price

What are the important points in a farm and ranch contract and how should you start? First of all is the price. As mentioned earlier, the asking price is never the taking price; there is always some room for negotiation, if not in actual dollars, then in minerals, access, equipment, or financing. Assuming the asking is reflective of the market, meaning it is based on comparable sales plus some margin for negotiation, you should initially offer at least 85% of the asking. Now, a lot of the time, the asking price is market plus 20% or 30% and offering 80% of that would result in your over-paying for the ranch. This is an area where your Broker should earn his pay. Your Broker should have knowledge of the market in the region of the ranch and should be able to advise you as to the validity of the asking. Your Broker should also have a feel for the amount of leeway in the asking price. You really don't want to sour the deal by offering a price that is ridiculously low. This really can insult the Seller and taint the whole deal, even kill it outright. As long as you feel the asking is fair, offering 85% of that is a good starting offer.

A Seller's options are to accept your offer, counter your offer somewhere between his asking and your offer, or reject it. Any way he responds, you'll learn something about his thinking.

If the Seller accepts your offer, move on and don't "second-guess" your offer. A lot of time, people buy places and anguish over the price after the fact. Do your homework, make the offer you can live with and move on. If the Seller rejects your offer, you have the option of raising the bid incrementally until you reach an agreed price or you hit your limit. If the Seller counters, the fun begins. A counter means you have the Seller's attention and have a chance to buy the ranch. Do not make a common mistake by always going halfway between the counter and your offer. If you feel the counter is still way too high, just come up a little. If the counter is fairly close to what you expect to pay, raise your offer most of the way to show good faith, reserving some cushion for further negotiations. If you hit an impasse on price, look for options in equipment, minerals, and payment terms, etc. that make the deal better for you without running the Seller off.

What if the asking is far above what the ranch is worth?

Sometimes the Seller is not well served by his Broker or decides himself what he wants/needs to get for the ranch. In those cases, if the market and the property simply do not justify the asking price, offer 90% of what you think it is worth. It may well sour the deal, but it may buy you a ranch if the Seller has not had any other offers and realizes that the market simply does not support his price. If a property is over-priced, you can sometimes make your offer and let it "sit". This serves to let the Seller know you want the place, at your price. Certainly, clear this with your attorney, but I don't like open ended offers. Put an end date on any offer, no matter how low, so there is a date after which the offer is withdrawn.

Earnest Money

Earnest money is part of the negotiations. In principle, the purpose of this money is to offset out of pocket expenses incurred by the Seller prior to closing in the event the sale does not close; normally the cost of the survey plus the title policy. The money is not paid to the Seller unless the deal fails to close due to something the Buyer does or does not do. Should the deal not close due to actions on the part of the Seller, the earnest money is returned to the Buyer. It has always served the purpose of showing good faith or the "earnest intent" of the Buyer as well. Because there is a chance the Seller will get the money if the buyer fails to close the deal, a large offering of earnest money serves to make the Seller feel more confident about your intentions. On a $1 million deal, an offer of $25,000 is acceptable, $50,000 is better.

Survey and Title Policy

As mentioned above, the survey and title policy is normally a cost paid by the Seller, but who pays these costs is fully negotiable. A new survey is recommended if the current survey is more than five years old or if significant work has been done on perimeter fencing. Certainly, a new survey is indicated if the tract is being cut out of a larger tract, or combining two or more tracts. Surveys are getting much more accurate, but because of new requirements put on surveyors by the State, to make the new survey reflect all the adjoining surveys, they take more time to do. Field work used to take two weeks and office work another week. Now, with GPS, field work takes a day, but office work takes a month. Providing the surveyor with the previous survey, deeds, and the farm and ranch contract will speed things up. It also helps if a copy of the title commitment is provided to the surveyor when it becomes available. However, as the surveyor now has to check that his survey matches all surrounding surveys, allow at least 30 days for the survey. This is normally how the date for closing is arrived at; 30 days to make a new survey and 15 more for the Buyer/Seller to review the survey.

The title policy is very important and money well spent. While I have never heard of someone contesting title after a purchase, it could happen and the title company is supposed to provide insurance to the Buyer to protect him/her from that. In truth, the real value of getting a title policy is the title commitment. This is a document that the title company issues to all parties that reflects all instruments of record that might affect the title to the subject property. Old oil leases, mineral divisions and reservations, easements, mortgages, etc. are all researched by the title company and set out in the title commitment. This is an excellent example of spending a little to save a lot. Be sure to provide the title commitment to your attorney for his review. Objecting to issues in the title commitment is a favorite pastime of real estate attorneys but important to the Buyer. Because some of these issues can be easily removed at this time, it is a great opportunity to "clean up" the title. It is also your last time to learn if there are any serious restrictions to your use of the land. Mineral rights are mentioned as recorded reservations and leases, but are not insured and not really well delineated. It will take an attorney to determine what mineral rights you will really receive at closing. This in itself is enough reason to ask for a title policy. When minerals are important or if your new ranch is in a mineral-active area, it might be a good idea to have a mineral search done at your expense. As mentioned, with the new O/G activity in Texas, landmen are more prevalent and more reasonable. Within a week you will know who owns what and what activity the ranch has seen over the years.

Another real service the title company provides is the preparation of the documents required for the transfer of ownership. Usually the title company prepares the deed, the mortgage, and the closing statement, which outlines who paid what in the closing. They also actually "close" the deal; making sure all parties sign what needs to be signed and that funds are properly distributed. Closings are complex, tedious chores and you should come to appreciate your closer.

Minerals

While on the subject, what minerals do you ask for? Initially, the minerals offered should have been outlined in the prospectus. If, as is often the case, the percent of the mineral estate to be conveyed to the Buyer is "negotiable", ask for all owned minerals as this is a negotiable item. Do not expect a low price and all the minerals unless the Seller is very motivated, but start out by asking for all and negotiate down if given the chance.

If owning some portion of the mineral estate is critical to you, state specifically that you will receive some portion of the minerals. Do not ask for "half of all owned minerals" because if it turns out the Seller doesn't own any, you get half of nothing. No, state specifically that you will receive "one-half" or "one-fourth" or "ten percent" of 100% of the mineral estate. Then, if the Seller owns less then he thought, you have leverage and an out, if you choose to exercise it. If the Seller offers a portion of the minerals, spell out that offering in the contract so the deed will reflect it. Never assume that the Seller really understands what minerals he owns. As discussed earlier, the mineral estate can be divided into five separate rights. A Seller my think he has all the minerals when in fact, he only owns all the executive rights or all the royalty rights. Make everyone concerned be specific and ask questions, addressing all parts of the mineral estate. Like minerals, water rights and now wind rights can be important. Ask for 100% of both.

Other Conveyances

In addition to the land and the fixed improvements, often-times equipment is conveyed as part of the deal. Tractors, deer blinds and feeders, camping trailers, even windmills sometimes disappear between the agreement and closing. Anything you think you're getting as part of the ranch should be listed some-where in the contract, even if you have to add an addendum. A very smart client of mine, when he was selling his ranch, refused to include any equipment in the negotiations. His opinion, which is now mine as well, was if you include equipment in with the land, you do not get any value for it. Conversely, if you are the Buyer, unless specifically asked not to, ask for all the rolling stock, all the farm equipment, all the blinds and feeders, certainly all the water systems, gates, and furniture. Assuming you've made a reasonable offer, the worst thing that can happen is the Seller will cross it out.

Addendums

Both the Texas Real Estate Commission and the Texas Association of Realtors have formulated addendums which can be added to the basic contract. Ask your Broker for a list of the addendums to see if any apply to your deal. At a minimum, I always include the environmental addendum which gives the Buyer the right to have inspectors study the property for toxic substances, endangered species, or wetlands. A basic assessment, called a Phase 1 Environmental Inspection, should run about $2,500 and is a good investment on any property that has a history of intensive farming (banned chemicals), oil and gas production, or might have either endangered species or wetlands. Other addendums often found in farm and ranch contracts include Seller Financing, Property Condition (when the housing is a significant part of the price), and the addendum concerning lead based paint (for homes built before 1972).

Miscellaneous Items to Consider

In the excitement of buying or selling a ranch, sometimes things get overlooked that lead to conflict. It is possible, and far better, to get these things spelled out early on, preferably in the contract. The first is access prior to closing. The Seller often has a lot of work to do before closing, moving cattle or equipment, and he may be sentimental about selling the place. On the other hand, the Buyer is anxious to get to know his new ranch and start making improvements. Therein lies a potential wreck. Access to the ranch prior to closing should be set forth in the contract and include provisions for inspections as well as tours by the Buyer. If this period occurs during the hunting season, it is normal for the Buyer's access to be limited to weekdays and it is normal to require the Buyer to notify the Seller when he wants access. But the issue should be addressed and in writing.

Hunting leases and grazing leases are also potential problems. I am in the process of closing a ranch that is leased through the hunting season and, while closing is set for after the season, Buyer access may cause a problem with the hunters. For now, visits to the ranch by the Buyer are limited to Monday thru Thursday, 10 AM to 3 PM. Grazing leases are simpler and usually end with closing. However, since no one wants to move their cows until it is certain that the ranch is sold, they are usually given 30 days after closing to remove their livestock. Likewise, since the Seller really doesn't want to move out until the place is sold, there is usually a similar period of grace for him/her to remove personal effects. Lastly, if the Seller is involved in any government programs such as the Conservation Reserve Program, he must notify the proper governmental agencies that he is selling the property. The Seller should also be directed in the contract to provide the Buyer with copies of all government agreements and leases, anything that will survive closing.

The Option Period

While on the subject of access after the deal is made, a relatively new clause in the Farm and Ranch Contract is the Option Period. This is a period of time, fully negotiable, that gives the Buyer a "free look" at a negotiable fee. During this period, the Buyer usually has unlimited access to the property for himself and his agents/inspectors with notification of the Seller or his agent. This period is when you do the Phase I, dig potential pond sites, census deer, etc. As written, the Buyer can walk away from the deal for any reason during this period. If the fault is something the Seller can remedy, he can do so, but is not obligated to do so. Likewise, the Buyer has no obligation to explain his decision to walk away. Option periods are usually for two weeks and usually can be established for ½ of 1% of the purchase price.

Actions Before and After Closing

Once you have reached an agreement with the Seller and the contract has been receipted at a title company, there are several actions you need to monitor. First of all, ensure that a surveyor has been retained and has all the documentation possible to do his job. Even if the Seller is paying for the survey, your Broker should follow up on this, and may be asked to show the surveyor the ranch initially. Also, if you are borrowing the purchase money, your financial institution will require an appraisal of the property. Set up a tour of the ranch for the appraiser early on and be sure he/she is aware of any comparable sales you used in your determination of a fair market price. Bank appraisers often are not experienced in every area of the state and welcome assistance in gathering supporting data. Agricultural lenders, like Capital Farm Credit have appraisers working different areas so are usually on top of values. Point out any aspect of the property that makes it more valuable to you, the brush, the wildlife, or a big lake for instance. You want the loan to come through, and a higher appraisal makes the loan more attractive, more "do-able".

As mentioned, go by the power company and the phone company and fill out the paperwork for a smooth transition of those accounts. Visit with your insurance provider, or seek out a rural insurance provider so you will be covered the day of closing. Make a point to visit with the Natural Resource Conservation Service and let them know you are the new owner. There may be a conservation plan in effect, one that might suit you as well with a few modifications. These are good people and they are eager to help. Always make appointments if you want their undivided attention as they may switch offices during the course of the week and are very busy. One of the valuable services they offer is an approved contractors list. This is a list of earthmoving companies, custom farmers, well drillers, etc. all the trades you might need to set up your ranch. While they do not guarantee nor endorse these contractors, just being on the list means these contractors have some validity. Visit with those you think you might need in the future to get an idea of prices and availability.

If you plan to run livestock, visit with the county agent as well as the local livestock commission company. Start accounts at the feed store, the lumber yard, the hardware store and the propane company if applicable. Some of these accounts take time to get up and running and you'll appreciate the convenience of uninterrupted service.

In addition to the environmental inspection, make arrangements for a house inspection if the house is a significant part of the purchase or if you plan to live there more than on weekends.

While on the ranch, spend some time learning the roads and the fencing system as well as any water systems. Some people have a hard time learning a ranch if they're used to street signs and 90 degree turns. I find that simply driving helps at first followed by walking those areas not accessible

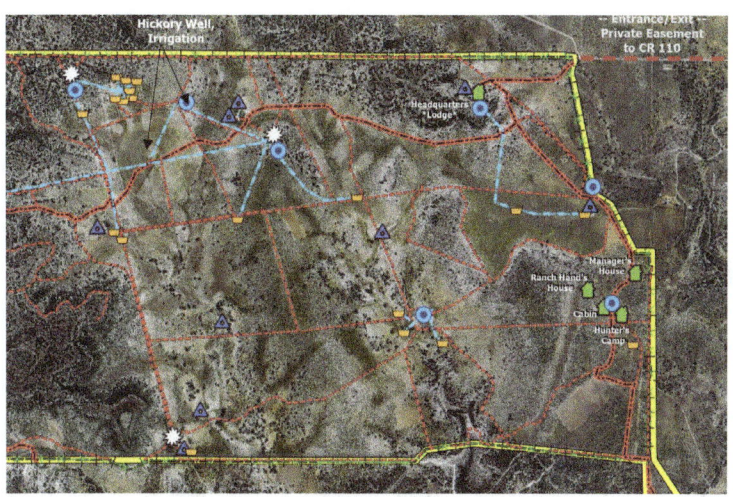

*Start marking maps with improvements/features to
familiarize yourself with the lay of the ranch.*

by vehicle. An ATV or horse can be very useful in this phase
of the process.

Once you feel comfortable with your directions and the
lay of the ranch, start a mental inventory of the flora and
fauna. Divide the ranch into segments using roads or fences
and spend time learning what the brush composition is, the
forbs and the grasses. Learn distances from water and what
the dependability of that water source may be. By this point,
you should have your water samples back and can pinpoint
good water and inferior water sources. In established fields,
take soil samples and submit them for testing to determine
fertilizer needs, if any. While on the subject of soil, this is the
perfect time to compare the maps you downloaded from the
Web Soil Survey with what you see on the ground.

Assuming you can do so without conflicting with hunters
or the landowner, set up trail cameras and feeders of your own
to start getting an idea of the deer and feral hog population
if that interests you. If you're a bird man, learn the preferred

bird foods and assess their abundance or lack thereof. Listen for quail calling and seek out turkey roosts. Spend time *at* the ranch *out on* the ranch.

After a smooth closing, your first stop should be at the county tax appraisal office. Let them know you are the new owner of the such and such ranch and ask for their form to transfer the agricultural valuation for ad valorem taxes (the ag "exemption"). Their office will be notified by the county clerk when the transaction is filed for record, but just in case there is a screw-up, be proactive and get the paperwork started immediately. If the ranch you've just bought is valued for agricultural purposes for ad valorem taxes for wildlife management, ask for a copy of the management plan. If such a plan has been prepared, it will be a source of valuable information. By the same token, if there is an NRCS conservation plan for the ranch, even one designed for livestock, it will have some useful information. Gather all available input on this piece of ground you just bought, learn the lay of the land, and begin preparing your development plan.

Section 2

PREPARING YOUR RANCH
DEVELOPMENT PLAN

What Is a Ranch?

Now that you own a ranch, what is a ranch, what is it you own? A ranch, be it 10 acres or 10,000 acres is a living machine. It takes in moisture and sunlight and converts them into food, food for animals, insects, and plants. Such a machine is known as an ecosystem. A square foot is a huge ecosystem for microbes, a square mile is an ecosystem for a Whitetail buck, and a hundred square miles is an ecosystem for a Mountain lion. Whatever that organism needs to survive and reproduce must be available somewhere in the system or the organism must leave or die out.

How many individuals and how many species can exist in an ecosystem is determined by space and the richness of the system, how much energy it can produce, given the weather, soils, and current occupants. This concept is called the carrying capacity. Carrying capacity as applied to animals is the number of animals that a given tract of land can support in a healthy fashion. At or below carrying capacity, a population, be it wood rats, elephants, or deer, should be able to obtain adequate nutrients in the wild to reproduce, rear their young, and realize their genetic potential. Populations above carrying capacity will experience smaller body weights, a drop in reproduction, increased natality

Every ranch is different, every ranch an ecosystem onto itself.

(death of young), and in the case of Whitetail deer, smaller antlers. Carrying capacity varies from place to place, and varies over time on the same place. It is a function of time, weather, soils, animal densities (consumption), vegetative diversity and succession. It is easily influenced by the actions of Man. Estimating carrying capacity for any species is difficult at best, and is most accurately determined by judging body condition of individuals and reproductive success of the population over time. Your ranch has a carrying capacity which will dictate to some degree its' potential, whatever your management objectives.

Speaking of which, what are your management objectives? You should have some idea at this point what you bought the ranch for. It can be any number of things including trophy deer, great fishing, or blue ribbon cattle. The majority of ranch buyers today are primarily interested in managing for Whitetail deer. A few are more interested in Bobwhite quail than deer, and a tiny fraction of the people buying ranches still see livestock as the primary reason they bought a place. These purposes need not be mutually exclusive and a wise landowner seeks out management schemes that above all nurture the land. Take a moment to set your objectives down on paper so that, as you read the following pages, you can better design your management plan. If you need help, the Texas Agricultural Extension Service and the Natural Resource Conservation Service are two great sources. They provide hundreds of pamphlets on land management and are available to help you through the planning process. These are governmental agencies and provide their services at no charge. As mentioned earlier, they are spread pretty thin though, and you need to be patient. If your objectives are specifically directed towards wildlife, Texas Parks and Wildlife provides excellent advice on managing wild game. If anything, however, their field technicians are even more overloaded, and appointments are necessary.

The following are discussions on the different components of a ranch management plan to help you learn how the system works and what impact you can have on your new ecosystem.

Developing Your Water Assets

That living chunk of dirt with all its inhabitants that you just bought, now known as "The Ranch", can get along for a time without food, but not without water. Certainly, rainfall will replenish moisture in the soil, which takes care of the amoebas, worms and insects. Others, like snakes and Javelina, get by on moisture in the food they eat. But a good many of the animals, wild as well as domestic, need drinking water on a regular basis convenient to their "safe" areas. That is not to say that you need a drinking fountain every 50 feet, but water plays a crucial role in the health of your ranch ecosystem. Availability of water also determines distribution of wildlife over the ranch which in turn affects your carrying capacity. You can have excellent brush on one side of the ranch, but without accessible water, the deer may not spend much time there. Quail, too, are known to hang around water so accessible watering sources, even if not actually used by quail for drinking, help increase their utilization of all areas of your ranch. You must consider your water assets first, before brush work, high fencing, or even your new camp house.

As anyone who has driven the State knows, Texas varies

greatly in its vegetation. This is due in part to soils, but more so to moisture. Anyone who has been to Balmorrhea, Texas, can see what difference moisture makes. In otherwise desert conditions, lush fields are possible because of the natural spring there. At the State Park in Balmorrhea is a wetland sanctuary, made possible by the spring and offering welcomed respite to wayward waterfowl.

For the most part, Texas receives its' moisture in the form of rain. Along the coast and up into the Hill Country, rainfall is often the result of tropical depressions. Out in West Texas, rainfall may most often come out of the mountains of Mexico, while in far North and Northeast Texas; rain may be associated with fronts from Canada or the Pacific. All of these systems affect rainfall in Texas and you will soon become an expert on the influences which affect your ranch. In general, Texas has what is known as bi-modal rainfall, meaning rain comes twice a year, in spring and fall. This is important to ranchers because they know they need to have reserves for those periods when it simply is not going to rain. These reserves are usually kept in two forms, cisterns filled by wells and surface impoundments. I learned recently of one ranch in far West Texas where an 18,000 acre ranch is watered by a single water well! The well is distributed over the ranch using booster windmills and cisterns connected by miles of pipelines. Another ranch I consulted on had one well and it went bad during the summer. Because the ranch was high fenced, and did not have any surface water due to sandy soils, water had to be trucked in for wildlife until the well could be replaced, a period of several weeks. You should avoid scenarios like these and hopefully your research before buying has made the point moot.

How much water you need is an important question. For cows, I always allowed for 16 gallons per head per day during the summer. I held a two weeks supply on hand in cisterns just in case the well went bad. This was in spite of having several large stocktanks on the ranch. I recommend this because as sure as you don't have a reserve, the stocktanks will go dry and your well will crap out. Selling your herd at the peak of a drought is no fun and is hard on your bottom line.

I also distributed the water into each pasture, providing water at one-mile intervals. That way, cows did not have to travel further than one-half mile to water. This may well be overkill, but I learned that this helps to disburse the cows over the entire pasture, improving grazing. I'm sure you've seen those stocktanks that are devoid of all vegetation for 300 yards around. This is because it is only natural for animals to try and avoid any extra walking, preferring to graze as close as they can to their water source. Once that is all down to bare ground, then they'll forage out further. Adding water sources reduces this localized overgrazing. As an aside, I'll pass on another trick I learned from an old prof at A&M; he said to improve grazing distribution, place the salt blocks at the outer edge of their range, in this case at least one-half mile from the water source. Seeking salt, the cows will move out over the range and not camp out so much at the watering holes; something that works with wildlife feeders and supplementation as well..

What does all this cow talk have to do with you? You want to grow trophy deer or buckets of quail, not run cows, right? Well, water is perhaps more important to wildlife than it is to livestock because wildlife has to have water within its home range for that range to work. Remember, wildlife, be it deer, quail, or turkey, must be able to access water and feel safe while doing so. O.K., O.K., I know you're saying quail don't need drinking water and from pen studies, we know they can reproduce without free water, but can they rear their chicks?

Quail, particularly chicks, are very sensitive to heat, and surface water, through evaporation and the attendant green vegetation, can greatly reduce surface temperatures. Also, quail managers have observed that during periods of high temperatures and low humidity, quail will sacrifice security to get to water. Sacrificing security is something that simply does not happen in Nature without a reason. Trust me; you should plan for dependable, accessible water at least every mile across your ranch regardless of your management goals.

Surface Impoundments; Stocktanks

As mentioned, if you don't have a creek, spring or river, water is available from two sources, surface rainwater impoundments and subsurface water. Surface water is dependent on a non – or slowly-permeable soil unless you have a renewable source such as a spring. A client recently diverted the spring flow on his new ranch so he could improve a road only to see his lake melt away to nothing in a matter of days. This is one reason I place such an emphasis on soils when considering a ranch for purchase. If you do not have abundant subsurface (well) water, you must have good clay soils for impoundments or else you'll need to budget for numerous supplemental watering sources based on wells, storage tanks, and troughs.

If you do indeed have good clay soils, review your ranch on paper, measuring distances from surface water sources and drawing circles around each source using a one-half mile radius. Rate each water source from 1 to 3, with 1 being dependable year round, regardless of the weather, 2 being dependable with normal rainfall, and 3 being dependable during wet years. The circles rated as a 1 should very nearly touch across the ranch. Where there are gaps, you should consider adding supplemental water sources. I often recommend "pothole" tanks, a hole dug in a watershed just big enough to bury a suburban or truck. In clay soils, these are a good idea. Cheap to dig, they can be designed to afford excellent access cover for wildlife as the dozer need only come in and leave on one side, leaving three sides brushy. Because they are small but deep, they are ideal for supplementing with a well, even if it is a mile or more away, using poly pipe.

But potholes don't work well in sandy soils and do not have the longevity of a deeper stocktank. To fill a gap in your water system with an earthen stocktank, I think the minimum size would be 5,000 cubic yards in excellent clay, 10,000 cubic yards in anything less than pure clay. As discussed, any surface impoundment should be properly constructed, with a true coring of the dam and an assessment of the watershed. If your ranch is flat, you can sometimes use "wings" to gather water from several smaller drainages. I did that once near Big Wells and successfully put in a 10,000 cu. Yd. tank in a flat area that really needed dependable water. We "crowned" a long stretch of roadway, simply humping the roadway, and the resulting bar ditch served to collect runoff from several hundred acres even though there was not much in the way of a discernable drainage.

You should always try for depth over surface as your main loss after seepage will be from evaporation. In Medina Co., loss to evaporation as per the soils book is 60 inches a year. With an average rainfall of 28 inches, you can see that without significant runoff, you're finished before you start. I always try for at least 15 feet in depth, with a 1 to 4 slope on the sides. This will require the use of a "scraper" in addition to a dozer, so you should get a true stocktank contractor vice someone with a dozer alone.

Assessing the best site for a stocktank and the watershed that will feed it is tricky and best left to the agents of the Natural Resource Conservation Service. Variations in soil permeability, vegetation, and slope all affect runoff and thus the amount of water you will catch with a rainfall. The NRCS technicians are trained to asses these factors. Not only will they determine where you can build a stocktank and estimate the watershed, they will design the pit, stake the pit for your contractor, and measure the final hole. It's always nice to have a third party estimate the soil actually moved come time for payment.

As a very general rule, a 5,000 cubic yard stocktank is 90 feet by 90 feet and 15 feet deep with a 4:1 slope and requires 100 acres of good runoff, no sand, to be dependable. Currently, tank builders in my area are charging $4.00/cu. yd. to dig such a 'tank. While on the subject of earthmovers and land clearing costs, remember to try and lump as much of the work together as you can afford. That gives you some negotiating room with the contractor as it costs him a lot to move between jobs. Knowing he will have several weeks worth of work will make him more amenable to negotiations.

Existing stocktanks always have some silting which reduces their depth and may lead to increased seepage. Older stocktanks should be evaluated as to their current capacity and future potential. Cleaning an old stocktank is rarely possible, as to do so with a dozer or scraper the stocktank must be dry for at least a full year. Do not think that just because the surface of a dry stocktank is cracked and growing grass you can move in and clean it out. I remember one large lake that was so dry I could drive across even the deepest part of the old pit. However, once we got a dozer on it, the weight and vibrations broke the crust and turned it all to a sloppy pudding. We finally were able to clean it out with a wheeled front end loader at considerable expense. We justified the expense by deepening the pit and greatly enlarging the lake.

There are still some draglines out there, and there are some newer tracked backhoes that can reach out quite a distance from shore. If you have a small stocktank that needs cleaning, you might try and find a contractor with one of these machines. Otherwise, just dig a new pit downstream from the old one and leave the old one as a silt trap.

Leaky tanks are rarely worth messing with. Unless the tank is small enough for a plastic liner, and you have no intention of ever letting cows (or feral pigs) near it, I recommend moving on. It is unfortunate that rarely does time seal a leak; rather, time often makes the leak worse. In my dismal history at fixing leaking stocktanks, I have had no success with Bentonite or drilling mud. I may well have done it wrong, but it just has not worked for me. One stocktank I did fix had a certain soil that appeared to be good clay but would not hold water. Upon testing the soil in a lab, we found that the addition of plain salt would make it hold as intended. Again, the fine folks at NRCS saved my rear.

In sandy soils, stocktanks are a poor investment. Even if there is clay at deeper depths, you will have to seal the upper levels if you want the stocktank to ever be "full". Scaling the sides with borrowed clay is an art and chancy at best. As with liners, a stocktank once sealed with borrowed clay should not be used to water livestock as they will punch through the seal, negating the treatment. I recommend the liberal use of concrete or plastic basins in very deep sandy situations and have even used old satellite dishes as basins for turkey.

If you have a well, you can make a decent temporary dove pond using Bentonite on sand. Simply scrape out a long pit 40 yards by 20 yards with a max depth of 24 inches, pour in bagged Bentonite as directed and disk it in, retaining the bowl shape as best you can. Filling this pit two weeks before the season, and keeping water in it will draw any dove in the area. However, since it is so shallow, it will require additional water regularly because of loss to evaporation.

Concrete basins in sandy soils improve water conservation/availability.

Wells

If for whatever reason, your new ranch is not suitable for surface water impoundments, or if you want the security of dependable water at the flip of a switch, you need to maximize existing wells or consider drilling a new well or two. While not as aesthetically pleasing as a stocktank, this water is more dependable and can be just as effective for servicing wildlife and livestock. Water for livestock is pretty much cut and dried; you need a trough low enough for calves and a supply adequate to recover quickly from a herd-sized visit. That is why you often see cisterns at windmills or oversized troughs like the King Ranch uses. With a rate of 5 gallons per minute on a good mill, a herd of 30 cows will die waiting for a small trough to refill.

Of course, if power is available, I much prefer an electric submersible pump. They are reliable and even smaller pumps can produce great quantities of water if run 24/7. When basing your water system on an electric submersible pump, it is still

Tried and true, windmills also add romance to the ranch.

a good idea to include a reservoir which can hold several days' water in reserve, more if you cannot check on it often. It is a cruel fact that wells usually go down during drought and the well service company is usually swamped when they do. Please make allowances for such an event even if you think you have adequate earthen storage capabilities.

Solar pumps are an option when power is not readily available. In shallow wells, I have seen solar pumps provide more water than a windmill and solar pumps do not blow over when you're not around.

Recently, there has been a great increase in the use of the black plastic reservoirs. At about $900 for a 1,550 gallon tank,

Always have adequate storage to survive down time.

these are a great option. I know of one ranch in La Salle Co. where the landowner used a series of these plastic tanks to provide water for his headquarters and livestock. Well water there was extremely deep and it was uneconomical for him to drill a well. Instead, he had 20 of these storage tanks hooked together and he saved every drop of rain water that fell on anything with a roof. He lived on the place and raised deer, and always was able to get by with this system alone.

For wildlife, recovery rate is not as important since wildlife usually waters in small groups or singly. For wildlife, access is more important, as water that cannot be accessed with ease and some feeling of security is like not having water at all.

Trough height is a primary concern, as a trough accessible to an adult Whitetail may be too high for a fawn, and is simply a deathtrap to a quail. An inexpensive fix for this problem is to tap into the water feed line and run a short piece of PVC or poly pipe out to the nearest good cover. Add a drip valve to the end and wildlife of all sizes can safely water. If you have feral hogs, forget the PVC unless you bury it; PVC is a favorite toy for feral hogs. Just use poly pipe and tie it to a tree or stake six to ten feet from the end, and leave the end with the drip valve unattached. The hogs will of course play nose soccer with it, but usually will not damage it. If you choose to install a basin at the end, the lines should all be buried and the basin fenced.

Some people let their troughs run over to form a small mudhole. I don't recommend this, particularly if you have livestock, as the cows will over time remove a lot of dirt from around the trough in effect making it even harder for wildlife to access. If the well can produce enough water to do so, it is best to dig a small earthen pond adjacent to the well out in the brush. Run an overflow line from the storage tank to this pond and let the mill overflow keep it wet. If it is an electric well, you can install a float on the side of the pond (remember to fence it well), in effect making it a large trough.

The use of poly pipe in water distribution is arguably the greatest innovation in wildlife management since the root plow. Properly laid out, poly pipe can distribute water over great distances using gravity alone. If used with a pressure pump and storage tank, you can run water virtually anywhere. Currently, electrical power is running $5.50/ft. in my area, while 2-inch poly can be installed at $1.35/ft. You can see that, given a strong well, it is much cheaper to distribute that water than it is to dig another well and run power to it. Sometimes a well simply will not make much water at any given time, but can make water dependably. Such wells are still very useful if you add storage capability or adapt the well to interval use. On a recent job near Lytle, I had a weak well, but lots of power. I steam-cleaned an old oil storage tank and hooked it up to the well. From the storage tank, I added a booster pump and 35 sprinklers set out over 600 acres. The well was turned on and off with a float inside the storage tank and the sprinklers were controlled with a swimming pool timer. The sprinklers would come on and run for a period of time that would not quite drain the storage tank. The well of course came on when the level in the storage tank dropped and would continue to run until the float cut it off. Once the timer cut the sprinklers off, the well could catch up and the storage tank would be full for the next watering period. Costly and complicated, but it allowed us to accomplish our goal with a low-producing well.

Some poly pipe is resistant to ultraviolet rays and thus can be left on the surface, although I recommend burying any poly less than 2 inches in diameter. I don't know how they do it, but in the smaller diameters, rats and Javelina can smell the water and will cut the line into small segments to drink and, apparently, just for fun. Once this happens, the feral hogs move in and soon you have an unplanned mud hole and the cistern is dry. Speaking of dry cisterns, you should learn early on to check your water system(s) regularly if your ranch is dependent on well water. With or without a high fence, your animals depend on you for that water. Lastly, even in deep South Texas, wrap your pipes and well fixtures. An unexpected freeze can crack a pipe, burning out the pump, and draining the cistern, leaving your animals out of water until your next visit.

Managing Vegetation

I'm sure you've heard it said that nothing is constant in Nature. Your piece of Nature is no exception and is constantly changing, even though day to day it may appear to be the same. Some changes are relatively rapid, such as grass growing. Others are slower, such as the filling of a pond with silt. But every day is a full work day in Nature and with or without your influence; your ranch will be constantly changing.

Before European Man got here, Texas was a much different place with much different vegetation. Vast grasslands, verdant, dark forests, and gently rolling hills covered with deep, rich soil. All this has been changed over the last 200 years by us, slow learners at best when it comes to managing ecosystems. Because of our predecessors, gone are millions of tons of topsoil, millions of acres of protective turf grasses, and thousands of trees, lost forever. The people that caused this loss were for the most part not evil, not greedy, just ignorant. They did not know Texas, its weather, soils, and vegetation, and tried to draw from what seemed to be unending resources as if they would last forever. We know now that without wise use, they will not.

Texas remains primarily a privately-owned state which is a good thing for the most part. What is bad about private lands are landowners that do not learn from others, do not seek better ways to manage, and do not benefit from mistakes of the past. Hopefully, you will not be one of these. Do not let this simple book be your last and only reference. Continue to seek new and better ways to manage your ranch and research before you commit. One area where this is of primary importance is in management of vegetation on your ranch. What you do to the vegetation, whether it is simple mowing, deep root plowing, or just looking the other way will have ramifications affecting the whole system. With that sermon done, a review of vegetation management techniques is perhaps in order.

Herbaceous Vegetation

In our earlier discussion of plant succession, I mentioned that weeds were the first stage of succession following soil disturbance. Weeds are herbaceous vegetation, as are grasses and the term simply implies that they are plants without woody stems. Not to confuse you, but grasses can be part of any stage of succession, including the climax or final stage of succession. Think of the vast prairies; without the influence of Man, those grasslands existed for thousands of years, "managed" by fire and grazing buffalo. Because weeds and some grasses are plants of early succession they are shallow-rooted, without woody stems, and as a rule, more easily managed. Many herbaceous plants are annuals, meaning they sprout, grow, and die in one year or growing season. Others, some grasses for example, are perennials, meaning they live for several years.

The first type of management technique is mechanical, whereby the plants are physically manipulated. This class includes mowing (shredding), disking, plowing, and roller-chopping. These treatments give immediate visual control of the plant and thus are selected by many because of the immediate gratification. I favor disking because it not only removes vegetation; it turns the soil and starts the successional clock again at Stage 1; mowing does not. Roller-chopping can turn the soil as well, if the implement is heavy enough and the soil is loose enough. Plowing, on the other hand, sometimes turns the soil too deeply, placing the weed or grass seeds too deep in the soil, setting the clock too far back or introducing a whole new seed source. Mowing or shredding of herbaceous plants does little but stimulate new growth, much like the grass on your lawn.

The next type of management techniques involves the use of chemicals. Chemical management of herbaceous vegetation is as old as farming. Surprised? C'mon, fertilizing a crop with manure is nothing more than adding chemicals to the soil to increase soil nutrients to improve plant vigor. Fertilization has a role to play on your ranch as well for the same reason, to reinvigorate tired soils. Of course, when we think of chemicals and herbaceous vegetation, we think of their traditional use, using herbicides to kill or control unwanted plants, much as you would in your yard. However you decide to use chemicals in herbaceous plant management, you need to know that however good they may be, they are not precise. Fertilizing corn also feeds sunflowers and killing grass burrs may also kill croton (dove weed). Here again, it pays to ask questions, read the label, and test your application on a small area to see if it does what you want.

You also need to remember that Nature can throw you a curve at any time. I remember one time I fertilized 125 acres of winter wheat south of Charlotte (Texas, of course). The wheat sprouted then shriveled up, but we had the prettiest damn crop of native sunflower that fall. Poor grazing of course, but some really great dove hunting! This was due to a combination of factors. I turned the soil in the fall, which incidentally promotes native sunflower. Then I fertilized the soil, ostensibly for winter wheat. Nature stepped in with a light rain which sprouted the wheat but failed to follow up with additional rain, thereby killing the sprouts. Native sunflower, on the other hand, really doesn't come on until January or February, so it was perfectly poised for spring rains and did very well in the absence of any competition.

Easily the most obvious form of herbaceous plant management is the use of livestock to consume grass and weeds. Texas is still cow country, and everyone who has 10 acres has to have a cow. I read one time that 95% of the cattle herds in Texas were smaller than 25 animals. I would think that is even truer today, with the fragmentation of rural land.

Unfortunately, while grass does well being seasonally grazed off, many landowners do not realize that grass needs time, water, suitable temperatures, and soil nutrients to recover. A pasture that easily feeds 30 cows in April may not be able to support a rabbit in August. Grasslands in the U.S. evolved with periodic grazing by buffalo and the occasional wild fire. After grazing or fire, the grass was left alone until it could recover enough to either carry another fire or attract a herd of buffalo. With the arrival of European Man came fences and herding of domestic livestock which forced cattle to remain on land long after the surplus grass was grazed off. This caused the cows to graze closer, to "crop" the grass plants to the roots, killing the grass and allowing woody plants to sprout and become established.

Modern theory on cow-calf grazing management centers on rotating the herd through multiple pastures, removing only the surplus grass. Once the surplus grass is gone, the herd must be removed; either to another system of pastures or to the sale barn. Along the same lines, grazing with steers

"Nature's Lawnmower" is a great tool for managing herbaceous vegetation.

puts a lot of animals on a pasture or pastures, removing them when they have removed the surplus. Whatever the system, prudent grazing leaves healthy grass plants intact, ready to receive rainfall and recover.

Fire remains a sound management tool, although concerns about air quality and global warming tend to restrict its use in the more populated counties. Depending on the season of the burn, and subsequent rainfall, burning can increase grass and decrease weeds or increase weeds and decrease grass. I love fire as a tool, but caution the landowner in its use. Both the NRCS and Texas Parks and Wildlife are working to increase the number of qualified personnel who can advise landowners

Prescribed burning is an excellent tool if applied by a professional.

about burning. Look into becoming a certified Burn Master if you have the time and equipment. Excellent results can be cheaply attained if burns are properly planned and liability can be minimized.

Woody Vegetation

Managing woody vegetation is by definition, harder than managing herbaceous vegetation because you have a tough, sometimes flexible stem or trunk to contend with. Additionally, woody plants have deeper, more extensive root systems and some, like mesquite, have what are called "taproots", which go straight down and are hard to kill.

Management of woody vegetation is divided into two classes, top-removal and root-kill. Tools of top-removal include shredding/chopping/mowing, "stacking" which is simply piling up the tops with a dozer, chaining, which involves dragging a chain or cable over the brush, herbicides that kill the tops, fire, and goating, the use of goats to reduce the tops. Root kill techniques include repeated top removal treatments, root-plow-ing, herbicides, very hot fires, and deep disking, usually in two directions.

The battle with woody vegetation reads like a bad novel. Once kept in check by fire and competition with strong prairie grasses, woody plants, once established, are very difficult to eradicate. In some circles, technicians have even given up on the word "eradicate", preferring to call it brush "management" instead.

Not considered a problem until the 1930's, brush came under attack following WW II with the invention of tracked crawlers, the predecessor of today's dozers. Using two of these tractors connected by a heavy ships chain or cable, the plan was to simply knock mesquite trees over, allowing moisture to reach the grass and restoring the forage for cows. Problem with this technique was mesquite has a taproot. Removing the top did not kill the roots, and the plant simply sprouted from the roots at a point just below the surface. The resulting plant was worse than the original because it had multiple stems instead of just one. Instead of going straight up, this new-improved version branched out sideways. It was also a stronger plant, as it had the roots of a tree feeding a sapling. Repeatedly removing the top did nothing to the plant and did not restore grasslands.

With bigger, stronger tractors came the root plow. This technique involves pulling a horizontal blade under the surface, below the sprout zone on the roots, cutting the sprouting zone off and killing the tree/bush. This process is usually preceded by stacking, piling of the top matter off to the side, to make plowing easier. To be effective, root-plowing should be followed by raking, where a huge rake is pulled through the field, pulling up the severed root tops, preventing them from sprouting. Lastly, to be truly long-lasting, the whole process should be followed by hand gathering the stumps and sticks for burning. Properly done, the effects of root-plowing can be seen for about 14 years. It costs about $240 per acre, but I don't know of anyone who will hand pick the stumps anymore, so the effectiveness today is somewhat reduced. Naturally, it does not work a well in rocky soils, and may be overkill if your problem plant does not have a taproot. I know cedar, or blueberry Juniper, which is the bane of central Texas, is easily controlled by simple stacking. Cedar does not have a taproot and does not re-sprout. Removing the top in any fashion kills that plant.

Following the failure of chaining, and trying to avoid the costs of root-plowing, the next tool used against brush was chemical. Agent Orange, then known as 2,4,5-T, alone or with diesel, was very effective against brush and was sprayed over large areas of Texas to control a wide range of brush species. Rumors of 2,4,5-T being a possible carcinogen caused it to be taken off the market following Vietnam. I believe the rumors have been confirmed, as my brother died from cancer attributed by the Department of Defense to Agent Orange. I mention this not to dramatize his passing, but as a warning to you to be careful around herbicides, even those everyone thinks are "safe".

In place of 2,4,5-T, a host of herbicides have come on the market. These herbicides are more selective and do not contain the agents which made 2,4,5-T carcinogenic, to the best of the manufacturers' knowledge. I use herbicides in brush management, but I employ professionals to apply them and I avoid the area until the effective life of the herbicide has passed. One herbicide I like is called Spike and is herbicide in pellet form. Just to give you an example of herbicide application, Spike can be flown or broadcast on a brush patch at a measured density. The pellets sit there until it rains and the rain melts the pellets, taking the active ingredient down to the roots. Spike is effective against a wide range of woody plants but kills herbaceous plants as well for at least one growing season, often two.

Other herbicides are applied in liquid form, either to the trunk or the foliage. The expected reaction of the plant is defoliation. This is followed by new leaves and defoliation again. This process eats up stored food in the roots and if severe enough, will kill the plant. Expected kill with today's herbicides range from 40% to 80%, depending on a multitude of factors including weather, temperature, time of application, and amount absorbed. We used to think the best time to treat brush with herbicides was spring, when the new leaves came out. The thought was applying it then would improve absorption by getting the herbicide in before the leaves put on a waxy outer coat. Currently, most foliar herbicides are applied in summer, using a surfactant to defeat the outer coating and entering the plant when it is already stressed by heat and drought. Basal application, where the herbicide is applied to the trunk, is just as effective, perhaps more so, but is labor-intensive over large tracts. Applying herbicide to the trunk increases the effects of the herbicide and reduces collateral death to other plants.

Mechanical tools to treat brush continue to evolve as well. Shredders are now available that can remove the top of a large tree. The hydro-axe is an example. Mounted on a large tractor with solid tires, the hydro-axe, using a rotary shredder or spinning drum on hydraulic arms, "eats" trees and brush down to ground level. Able to clear 5 acres per hour in light brush, it is priced competitively with stacking and herbicides. Another example is the Browns Tree-cutter. Simply a shredder on steroids, the Tree-cutter can shred anything you can drive over, and bigger trees if you back it up over them. Smaller shredders can remove light brush at decent speeds and can be pulled by your tractor.

The roller-chopper was developed a long time ago and is still used today. This implement consists of a large drum or series of drums with blades welded longwise along the sides. Filled with water or oil for weight, and usually pulled by a dozer, the drums roll over brush and small trees, ideally cutting the stems and putting divots in the soil. These divots are a big selling point as they serve as catchments for rainfall which speeds recovery of weeds and grasses. Unfortunately, while very durable, roller-choppers often do not cut the stems, but simply lay them flat and crimp them. This leads to wild sprouting in thick mats which are hard to traverse and hard to kill with no increase in forage. Additionally, if the soil is too hard, or the brush stems too thick, the blades will not divot the soil and rainfall continues to run off. A variation of the roller-chopper is called the pasture aerator. Instead of straight, parallel blades, the pasture aerator has a series of six to 12 inch blades welded to the drums in a spiral. The thought was this would improve penetration and reduce the jerky motion of a roller-chopper which was hard on clutches and operators. Originally developed to control palmetto in Florida, the implement works very well in deep sand. It does not work well in hard clays or packed gravel, and does not have the cutting power of a roller-chopper. This is because the spiraling of the blades, while eliminating the choppy motion, also removed the forceful chopping action of a roller-chopper.

Planting Preferred Species

Having spent the bulk of this chapter on killing plants, I need to address planting preferred plants. Improved grasses, brush lines, and food plots are integral parts of ranch manage-

The Lawson Pasture Aerator is a form of a roller-chopper.

ment. As mentioned, most ranch buyers today are not buying their ranches to run intensive cattle operations. However, most ranches in South Texas have a history of cattle management and many have large fields, usually planted in "improved" grasses. Improved in this sense refers to a grass that, at least in theory, produces more forage than native grasses under similar circumstances. Carefully consider field management in your planning process. If you think you will have a cow-calf herd of some sort, fields are very important as a way to increase forages and rest your brush pastures. If, on the other hand, you are only interested in wildlife, fields should be treated as food plots and broken up if they are too large for wildlife to access. A significant part of my consulting services pertains to the reclamation of improved grass pastures for wildlife purposes.

If your new ranch has a large field or two in grass, you might consider taking action to make it more useable for wildlife. Using either physical disturbance with a disk or herbicides to reduce grass density, you can establish weed populations for wildlife. A prime offender that I encounter all the time is Coastal Bermuda grass. Coastal is a tough grass that produces a lot of forage in a variety of conditions. It is hard to kill out, but should be controlled as it tends to form a monoculture that is of little use to wildlife. Bufflegrass is another example. Overgrazing, disking, or burning will not kill a well-established grass. The only thing I have had success with is deep plowing in mid-summer following an application of Roundup herbicide. The Roundup weakens the plant, while the deep plowing exposes roots to the drying action of the summer heat. Even this treatment is not always a long-term solution and you must continue working the field to keep the grass at bay.

Once you have returned your fields to bare dirt or if you have a new field just cleared, you need to plan what you want to do with it. Failure to do so will eventually result in the loss of the field and the cost of reclaiming it once again. Most wildlife managers in Texas use their fields primarily as oat patches, to draw and hold deer during the season. Those with an interest in dove or quail prefer to plant the fields in small grains or manage for weeds which produce food for birds. In the next chapter, I'll address the management of fields as food plots as it applies to each species and ways to maximize what could be a major investment.

Managing Whitetail Deer

Over the course of 25 years in the wildlife consulting business, I have seen management emphasis change from cow-calf operations with deer leasing as an adjunct to pure deer programs with no cows and the agricultural exemption from ad valorem taxes granted for wildlife management alone. Whitetail deer are big business in Texas, all over Texas, not just in the "Golden Triangle" (Cotulla-Laredo-Eagle Pass). Management philosophies vary with objectives, and are evolving quickly, so rather than try to provide you with a deer management course this chapter will review basic deer management integrated it into sound ranch management planning.

As most ranch buyers today are primarily interested in managing for Whitetail deer, I thought it appropriate to begin our planning process with management considerations for deer. For those hoping to raise exotics, remember that good management practices for Whitetail deer are applicable to most exotics, keeping in mind that Whitetails and exotics often compete for the same foods. Do not make the common mistake of thinking that since many exotics consume a great deal of grass they are to be counted as cows. All exotics compete

A new version of the spin-cast feeder sits on the ground and is safer to fill.

to some degree with native wildlife and should be included in estimates of populations and carrying capacity.

Whitetail deer are currently managed at several levels of intensity in Texas. The first level is basically no management, where deer are harvested primarily for meat, with a preference for bucks. Supplementation consists of corn distributed using a spin-cast type feeder during the hunting season.

The next level of management consists of informed harvesting of both does and bucks, with an effort to improve herd dynamics. Supplementation consists of the corn feeders mentioned above with perhaps several small food plots for cool season forages; usually oats.

The next level may or may not require a high fence and intensifies the herd management by harvesting specific numbers of animals broken down by age and sex. Efforts are made to estimate herd numbers and herd composition and records are kept of the harvest, weather, and management actions taken.

Usually, supplementation is a combination of corn feeders with oats patches, and the goal is to maintain herd density at or below carrying capacity.

The next level includes high fencing, a planned harvest based on an informed estimate of the population, and cool season supplementation with oats or rye. This level of intensity adds additional supplementation of warm season forages (lablab, cowpeas, etc.) and/or bagged protein supplements. Efforts continue to maintain the herd at or below the carrying capacity of native food supplies, using the supplements to "boost" herd body condition to a higher level hopefully resulting in larger antlers.

The final level of Whitetail deer management is the "feedlot" approach. In this management scheme, deer densities are allowed to exceed carrying capacity with supplementation becoming subsistence. Usually seen in commercial hunting

*Providing dietary supplement as opposed to
bait is part of intensive deer mgmt.*

operations, it is a trade-off between income from more bucks with larger antlers and the feed bill. It often involves buying "better" genetics in the form of bred does or young bucks, and may include deer breeder pens to bolster deer numbers and quality.

Your development plan will depend on where you see your ranch on this scale, although you can certainly move up the scale over time as finances and herd quality dictate. For the purposes of developing your new ranch, specifically for deer, I will address the initial considerations.

How many acres do you need to accomplish your goals? That's entirely up to your level of comfort and finances. Admittedly, you cannot hunt ethically and have a trophy deer ranch on 5 acres, although it seems to be coming to that with all the pen-raised deer. But you can have a good deer program on a smaller place, even without high fencing. A doe in South Texas normally resides on a range of 300 acres; a buck, 600 acres. These numbers vary with the seasons and habitat quality, but gives you some idea. Knowing this, unless you buy more than 600 acres, your adult males will at some time leave your property, assuming free range, and others will come onto your property. This is not to say you cannot have quality deer on anything less than 600 acres without a high fence. It means that you should work to meet all of a deer's needs as best you can to reduce the need to wander. A concept called "sanctuary" is gaining favor. Using a sanctuary, you can hold deer on a smaller acreage as all their needs are met and the sanctuary is undisturbed most of the time. Minimum size of a sanctuary depends on density of cover, food/water availability, relative comfort levels of the deer, and overall noise/disturbance. Of course, deer move in and out of a sanctuary, but the concept is to make a safe home range much smaller than normal.

I have a good friend that lives in Illinois. He took a buck several years ago that made the Pope and Young Record book. He remains convinced that the deer lived in a small woodlot behind his house not only avoiding hunters for years, but meeting its' nutritional needs in a very small area.

To exist, deer require food, water, and cover. Meeting these requirements while maintaining suitable sex/age ratios will allow your deer herd to thrive. On native range, at or below carrying capacity, food is rarely limiting for deer. They are very adaptable and consume a wide variety of foods, changing food types throughout the year as different plants become palatable or "tasty". This is why diversity of plant species is so important when you are evaluating a ranch for purchase. It is important that you have chosen a property with a good selection of brush species and a good ground cover of weeds and grasses. So often, I hear buyers ask for "bull mesquite" or "blackbrush thickets" when describing their ideal ranch. This is a mistake if taken to extremes, as no one type or species of brush is ideal for Whitetail deer. You should always seek out a diversified mix of brush, forbs, and grass. Do not buy a ranch that is all guajillo or all whitebrush or all anything; you would have to supplement heavily to meet the total dietary needs of your deer.

O.K. let us assume you have purchased a tract of land with good diversity. How many deer should you have, or manage for? Remembering that deer will move on and off the property unless high-fenced; you should plan for no more than one adult deer for every 10 acres. This is an average density for native range in South Texas, and at this density without supplementation, antlers will not be maximized in most years. However, your estimate of the number of deer on your ranch; fenced or not, will always be low.

How *do* you estimate the number of deer "on" your ranch? Estimating populations is easily the most difficult part of managing wildlife. My very first wildlife professor, the late, great Dr. Sam Beasom, said the only time there was an accurate count of a deer herd was one time in Germany. Seems a fenced enclosure in the Black Forest caught fire and the entire enclosure was consumed, killing all the deer inside. Estimating the numbers of that herd then became a simple process of counting carcasses. Stories abound of attempts to count enclosed populations, with biologists going so far as to link arms and walking an enclosure, driving deer ahead or through their ranks. I once had to resort to driving deer in the Hill Country, where the herd, enclosed for many years had become nocturnal and would not move. We had to push through the thickets, running the deer out and across checkpoints where they could be counted. Regardless of the size of your ranch, regardless of whether it is high fenced or not, estimating your deer herd will be very difficult.

Techniques for estimating deer numbers vary. The most popular technique on larger tracts involves the use of helicopters. Helicopter counts are fun, fast, and allow you to see a segment of the herd you might normally never see. However, they are not accurate; with estimates of error running as high as 60% on a good count. Ideally, helicopter counts are done in early morning, with the pilot flying parallel transects across the ranch. Distance between transects and the height and speed of the bird are adjusted for density of the cover and the reactions of the deer seen. What you count are deer caught out away from their preferred loafing cover. The noise of the helicopter scares them and they move towards the safety of the brush. If they are already in their preferred cover, or if they are not particularly frightened by the noise, or if, as sometimes happen, they are *too* frightened by the noise, they won't move and you won't see them. However, I don't want to discount helicopter counts altogether. They have value on certain ranches; those with open brush that are larger than 1,200 acres low-fenced or 400 acres high-fenced. Repetition is the key, making every attempt to duplicate the time, weather, personnel, and the aircraft each year. Over time you will learn how "wrong" or inaccurate this technique is on your ranch, allowing you to adjust and gain some useable data.

Another technique used on large tracts is spotlighting. Spotlighting uses a spotter with a light, a vehicle and driver, and a counter. To conduct a spotlight count, you first set a course across the property that samples all types of habitat, open fields, thickets, food plots, etc., while trying to avoid doubling back or getting too close to an area already counted. As you should set a route of at least five miles, obviously this technique works better on large tracts. Driving the route at a speed slow enough to spot and identify deer seen in the light, the spotter calls out what he or she sees and estimates the distance to the furthest deer. The counter logs in the deer by sex and age, and the distances. At the end of the count, the sum of the distances multiplied by the length of the track gives you the area counted. Note, this is just for the area counted, not the whole ranch. If you counted an area totaling 30 acres out of a 3,000-acre ranch, you multiply the deer numbers by 10 to get an estimate for the whole ranch. This method also improves with repetition, as the spotter(s) get better at discerning deer and the driver learns the route. The same people should run a spotlight count at least five times in a one-month period, preferably when the leaves have fallen. A key aspect is setting the route as you do not want to just drive from one oats patch to another and consider that a fair sampling. If need be, push some new roads to access all habitat types if you want this technique to provide useful data.

On smaller tracts, the Hahn Cruise technique is good, as it duplicates a spotlight count only on foot in daylight hours. Set a route that will put the rising or setting sun to your back. As you probably will not see many deer initially, walk it once in full daylight, stopping every 50 steps and estimating the distance to cover on both sides. The sum of these distances, multiplied by the total distance walked gives you the area counted. Walk this route several times at sunrise and at sunset over a one-month period and record the deer seen. You will be amazed how much your ability to move quietly and to see deer improves over time.

Spot counts can be very helpful in confirming the three survey techniques above. Spot counts involve recording the number, estimated age, and sex of deer at oats patches, feeders, or waterholes. This type of counting gives you some idea of relative abundance i.e. are there more deer or less deer than last time we counted? Unless you have a lot of oats patches or feeders, and have an observer at them all simultaneously, spot counting will not give you a very accurate idea of the total population. This is an area where trail cameras can be useful, recording what animals visit a feeder over the course of a day or week. Body condition, antler development, and reproductive success can be assessed on the hoof and used to set the initial harvest quotas.

Lastly, the best source of information about the deer herd is not derived from counting animals on the hoof, but by gathering data from harvested individuals. Dressed weight, body condition, and antler growth, when coupled with a good estimate of the age of the individual, tell you a lot about the general health of the herd. Yes, I know there is some error in estimating age with teeth, but it is still the best tool we have and everyone in camp should learn how to do it. Good records over several years are all a trained biologist (or an educated landowner) needs to determine herd health.

Antlers are the product of genetics, nutrition, and time. If any of these three factors are limiting, the deer will not produce "trophy" antlers. In my opinion, genetics across south and central Texas are rarely the limiting factor. More often, time and nutrition are the reason for small antlers. I get a chuckle out of buyers that purchase a ranch in good deer country, high fence it, then immediately go looking for pen-raised deer to buy so they can "improve" their genetics. They have not managed the herd inside the fence, so cannot know what genetics they have, what potential is already there. Before spending some serious money and potentially introducing a problem to your ranch, manage what you have first, then consider "improving" your genetics.

While on the subject, and it is a hot topic, let me say that introducing new genetics to a whitetail deer herd is not as simple as buying a new bull. A Whitetail buck is capable of "covering" or breeding up to 12 does, but rarely does so in the wild. This is because of the social and logistical problems involved with courting and covering more than one doe. Breeding in Whitetail deer is a strenuous process and is very hard on the buck. Add to this the stress and confusion caused by being dropped into an established social structure, and a new buck probably will not do much breeding the first season or two. Recent studies indicate that it is not the "dominant" bucks that do most of the breeding anyway. A study at the Kerr Wildlife Management Area found that in an enclosure, the breeding was done by the middle bucks, not the B&C buck. Adding five very expensive bucks to an established herd of a hundred deer, with forty to fifty native bucks, will not do much, if anything, towards changing the genetic pool.

Buying females are a better bet, as they fit in better and

*Native genetics, low-fenced ranch, selective harvest
and supplemental feed produced this buck.*

are usually bought already bred, so you get at least one offspring from an introduced doe. But just what genetics are you
introducing? Admittedly, the doe contributes genetically to
the antlers of her male offspring, but how do you know she is
carrying the genes for wide horns or drop tines, etc., whatever
characteristic you are hoping for, even if you know what she
was bred to? Simple answer is, you don't, regardless of how
well you know that deer's pedigree. No, unless you want to
buy a potential trophy just to shoot him later, initially work
on managing the deer you have, high fence or no. Once you
have maintained herd numbers at or below carrying capacity
for several years, culled the inferior antler types, and have the
sex ratio where you want it, if you are still are not satisfied
with the antlers, then you might consider genetics.

How is all this used in managing your herd? As mentioned,
in South Texas I'd start with an objective density of one adult

for every 10 acres if you feel comfortable with your population surveys. Failing that, I'd manage for good body condition, at least one fawn per doe, and respectable antlers, suitable to estimated age. Start by setting the sex ratio at 1.5 males per female. On most ranches, there is a surplus of does and these need to be removed. Which does should be removed is not important, although certainly if a mature doe can be visually discerned, that's a good candidate. It is more important to just harvest does, any doe, until you get down to no more than 1.5 females per male. Why the emphasis on does? Because deer are so prolific, they can overpopulate their habitat in a very short time. Remember, one buck can breed 12 does, so if you only have one buck and 12 does, you'll probably get at least 12 fawns. When you adjust the ratio of does to bucks down to 1.5 to 1 you reduce the number does and thus the number of fawns, which helps keep numbers down. Additionally, as you remove does, the average age of the female portion of the herd gets younger. First time does usually have a single fawn; while older does in good body condition normally have twins. Managing for younger-age females equals fewer fawns and less strain on the habitat.

It is important to be proactive in deer management since you can only harvest during the season. Try to keep your herd below the maximum, even in wet years. This is a mistake many wildlife managers make, they forget to allow for habitat conditions. It is a remarkable fact that, in a drought, while conditions may get harsh for deer, they continue to reproduce. Reduce your herd numbers in dry times, as the country cannot support as many animals as in periods of normal rainfall. However, I do not recommend the reverse, allowing more deer to live, in wet years. This always leads to a surplus when the rain stops, and the surplus is hard to remove. Whether you're managing deer, cows, or peacocks, always manage your ranch expecting drought and you will not get caught short.

I often see landowners actively controlling predators and I wonder why. Predators are part of a healthy system and while they may kill that potential B&C fawn, they normally do the herd (and you) a great service, clearing out the dead wood. Unless they become an obvious competitor with you for healthy mature deer, I think they have a place in any deer program. Dr. Beasom once spent a great deal of time and effort clearing predators out of a pasture in South Texas and found that deer numbers were really no different than in the adjoining control pasture. All that predator control did not seem to affect long-term numbers.

Supplemental feed for deer is growing in acceptance and complexity. Whereas oats patches and spin-cast feeders of corn were once considered intensive, now custom mixes of protein, fiber, and minerals are considered the norm. I believe it is always a good idea to have small cool season food plots distributed across the ranch. These plots, planted in oats or rye, allow the landowner to assess at least some portion of his deer herd and to harvest surplus animals in a setting conducive to clean kills even by amateurs. Start by researching your soils and look for soils rated fair or good for grains, legumes, and/or forbs. Failing that, plan your plots in drainages as the better soils naturally occur there. Food plots for deer need to be at least five acres in size, but not more than 30 for best use. I'd much rather have four 10 acre plots than one 40 acre field. Managing these plots for oats or rye is simple, requiring minimal equipment. If you do not have a disk and tractor, rent or borrow one from a neighbor, or employ a custom farmer. It is important that the soil be turned properly for you to get a good stand. Once turned, apply fertilizer if the field has tested low in Nitrogen, or has been neglected for more than five plantings. Using a grain drill will give you a better stand and would be worth the cost even if you have no other implements. A drill can be pulled by a truck following proper seedbed preparation. If you don't have a planter, simply broadcast the seed at a rate of 60 pounds per acre with a bumper feeder and drag a pipe or gate over the seed to cover it lightly.

There is an increasing use of warm season forages for deer such as lablab or cowpeas. These crops should be high fenced to allow them to become established and to recover after grazing. I once planted five acres of lablab out in an open field near Crystal City. It came up nicely and was about 12 inches tall when the deer finally realized it was food. Within two days it was gone, leaves, stems, roots, and all. If you have your plots high fenced, you can control feeding and give the plants time to recover from heavy use. Simply erect a high fence around the plot, using two panel netting on at least two sides. When you want deer to access the field, raise the bottom panel(s). Do not lower the top panels as that might split does from their fawns. Once the deer have grazed the crop down, clear the plot and lower the bottom panel back in place, ensuring you do not trap any deer inside. I like to include some brush inside the high fence so the deer do not feel exposed when entering the field. I also like to make these fields larger than simple food plots. The cost of fencing goes down with size as a significant part of the cost is corners and gates. Also, warm season crops over the drier parts of the state must be properly planted and tilled. Farming is easier and more economical in larger plots.

Feeders vary greatly and can be quite expensive. Supplying corn as bait is simple and I need not go into it. Supplementing your deer herd is a bit more complex and should be addressed. Adding nutrition to the diet of your herd can bring measurable benefits if done properly. Protein pellets have become very popular and are provided to deer in a multitude of ways. I prefer the Lamco feeder which uses a timed release mechanism hidden inside the feeder body. It can be set for any number of feedings and places the feed in troughs for consumption. Both the number of feedings and the amount fed can be adjusted. Using a trail camera, I have noticed that multiple feedings over the night results in a scheduled use by a number of deer vice groups of deer vying for feed at one or two feedings. Drawbacks include wasted, soured feed if demand drops off and it rains on surplus feed. These type of feeders need to be checked regularly as demand does vary over the year.

Conversely, there are any number of feeders that display feed continuously with some protection from the elements. I do not recommend this type of feeder unless for some reason you cannot check your feeders at least once a week. Free-choice feeders do provide feed to the herd in a dependable manner, but also feed a lot of non-target species, most notably raccoons and rats. I have pictures of a raccoon hanging upside down from one of these feeders, scooping feed out for his buddies on the ground. Feeder choice is one of personal preference and one you can experiment with.

Managing Your Bobwhite Quail

The second most popular species that buyers cite as their reason for buying a ranch for wildlife management is Bobwhite quail. Other quail species are just as tasty, just as sporting, but do not respond as well to management and certainly do not lend themselves to classic dog hunting as does the Bobwhite.

As a landowner/manager, you should already be aware that there is a crisis affecting Bobwhite quail. Bobwhite quail numbers are down, way down, across most of the bird's native range. Fortunately for us, Texas and Oklahoma are two strongholds for wild Bobwhite quail, although numbers in these two states are down as well. With Whitetail deer in everybody's backyard, coyotes attacking poodles on the back porch, and Canadian geese taking over golf courses, why the decline in quail? Well, since there is in place a task force of real quail experts hard at work on the problem, I won't pretend I have the answer. I can say, having listened to some of the taskforce members and read some of their findings, it appears that changes in land use are a primary cause for the decline. Quail simply cannot adapt as well as other species have.

What are these changes in land use and how does it apply to you? Perhaps it would be best to take a look back when Bobwhite quail were in their heyday and compare conditions then to now. Interestingly enough, Bobwhite quail were not plentiful in South Texas a hundred and fifty years ago, nor were they all that numerous in Central or East Texas, either. Their numbers rose with the fragmentation of vast expanses of forest or prairie into small family farms. Farming then was not nearly as efficient as it is today, with small fields, brushy fence lines, poor harvest techniques, and weeds mixed in with the crops. This patchwork landscape produced a variety of foods within easy flight distances to good cover and quail filled the niche. Bobwhite numbers exploded and quail expanded their range from the Deep South into the new settlements of East Texas, then Central Texas, and finally, with the encroachment of brush, into South Texas. South Texas did not have quail until it lost its grass simply because grassland prairie does not provide enough food or cover for quail.

Over time, improvements in farming, ranching, and forestry, with newer, bigger machinery, made small patchwork farming obsolete. Fields were combined to make them more economical to plow by removing the old fencerows, and mixed forests became pine plantations, monocultures of same age pine trees, ideal for the lumber industry. Hay meadows changed from 3 acres to 300 acres, and pastures were cleared and planted in improved grasses with brush chained, plowed, sprayed, and burned out of existence. For a small bird that depends on a mosaic of plant life; weeds, grasses, brush, and trees, the new agricultural was sterile and deadly. Add to this the explosion of surburban development, and it's no wonder Bobwhite quail are not doing well.

If you bought your ranch primarily for quail, your ranch

should be in an area of good native habitat. Modern farming practices do not encourage quail, although they can do well along margins of fields if there is enough cover left and a source of food. In native rangeland, quail can find woody cover from predation, can usually find sufficient food, and nest in tall bunch grasses or cactus when grass is scarce. Put simply, if quail are present when you buy your ranch, their basic requirements are being met. Once you close, there are a number of things you can do to improve conditions for quail, hopefully resulting in increased numbers. However, if there are no Bobwhite quail on your ranch, you screwed up; chances are poor that you can ever have a huntable population of native birds.

I recently visited with a landowner who had a ranch out near Junction. He had bought 1,000 Bobwhite chicks. They were delivered in brooder houses that provided food, water, and protected the chicks from the elements. Following directions to the letter, he eventually released the chicks into the wild and they all died. He did it again, 1,000 chicks, brooder houses, release, all died. He called me to tell him what he was doing wrong and I had to tell him he did not do anything wrong, he was simply in the wrong place. Sure, there *used* to be quail on that ranch, used to be quail throughout that area, but years of sheep, goats, and cattle had reduced the ranch to rocks and cedar. Additionally, his ranch was high fenced and he had stocked it with exotics. His combination of livestock, exotics, and general overgrazing had eliminated forbs (weeds) from the ranch, eliminating most food sources for Bobwhites. Even if those poor chicks could have found cover, and adapted to living in the wild, there was no food. Easy fix you say, put out feeders! Well, I can tell you I've been there and tried that. On a ranch near Bandera, I had an unlimited budget to produce huntable native quail populations. The ranch was high fenced and cleared of cedar, leaving a pretty park-like appearance of live oaks and short grass. The ranch produced exotics commercially for meat and the exotics had eaten every weed and fought over any new weeds that sprouted. I tried to increase quail numbers through feeders and by feeding the roads, but I never overcame the lack of native foods, nor the lack of nesting cover.

On my family place near Hondo, we used to have a lot of Bobwhite quail when I was young, but not anymore. What happened? Primarily, it was not a change on our place, but on the neighboring places. Adjoining ranches had changed hands and been fragmented. The new owners wanted to run hobby herds of cows and either cleared brush for improved grasses or overgrazed their places, so our ranch was surrounded by what to a Bobwhite quail was a parking lot, devoid of food or cover. As our place was only 300 acres, there was just not enough suitable habitat for our quail to recover when natural events decimated the population. We had become an island surrounded by dead zones for quail. This is important to remember. There is a minimum acreage that will support sustainable Bobwhite quail populations. The exact minimum acreage varies with the quality of the habitat and the occurrence of natural quail "disasters", but may be as large as 3,000 acres.

O.K., horror stories over, what can you do to improve quail numbers on your ranch? First of all, remember that a Bobwhite quail is only about the size of a beer can. The entire existence of the bird is spent on the ground with brief forays into the wild blue yonder, usually in response to the threat of death. To do well, a Bobwhite must have food throughout the year, several types of cover, and sufficient numbers to survive naturally-occurring die-offs.

As Bobwhite quail do not "overgraze" their habitat like deer or cows tend to do, monitoring quail numbers is not as important. To track relative abundance year to year, you can record call counts or covey rises during your travels over the ranch. With quail, however, the real inventory comes with the harvest as management cannot be judged effective unless it produces huntable birds during the season.

Management techniques for Bobwhite quail include regular disking to promote weeds, controlled grazing, burning, feeders and small food plots, and predator control. These actions are most effective when applied in a framework of suitable woody cover. Certainly, you do not have to manage your whole ranch for maximum utilization by quail. Some landowners manage the better soils, i.e. sandier soils, for quail by stripping the brush, and leave the brush on the heavier soils. In truth, most of the brush work we do for "quail management" is really to improve hunter access and success. Quail do pretty well in guajillo or shrub oak thickets; opening them up simply allows us to hunt them more easily. Of course, when we do open up thickets, it does increase the forb or weed segment of their diet, which is very important.

If quail hunting is a major concern, initial considerations when you take possession of your ranch should include a critical assessment of the relative percentage of woody cover to open areas. A long-held rule was 20% woody cover to 80% open. This is not a hard and fast ratio, but can be adjusted based on the density of the brush. I have learned thick brush growing close to the ground, like hogplum provides adequate cover for quail in strips as narrow as 5 feet. Conversely, regrowth mesquite, with little foliage near the ground, will not provide attractive cover for quail in strips 50 yards wide. And the 80% open country cannot be a monoculture of Bermuda or Bufflegrass. It can be grass, preferably a bunchgrass, and ideally should have strips or clumps of forbs across and thru it.

The best quail hunting I ever experienced was along old fencerows in the Valley on an abandoned fern farm. The fields were small, perhaps 300 feet across and full of good food plants for quail. The fencerows were very dense, but only 15 feet wide at their widest. This would equate to about 10% woody cover (150 feet of open/15 feet of brush). However, because the brush all along the fences provided good cover close to the ground, quail were able to escape to good cover easily and the weedy fields provided abundant food close to this cover. In one stretch we walked, representing perhaps 50 acres of total habitat, we busted 8 coveys of 15 birds or more, just walking the fences. So you can see it all depends what cover is available close to the ground and how dense the overhead cover is. While some taller woody plants are a requirement for quail to feel secure and to reduce ground temperatures, cover close to the ground is most important.

I have referred to clearing brush as "stripping", but you need not limit yourself to boring straight lines of brush. What we are going for here is edge and quail don't care if the edge is along a 500 foot strip, straight as an arrow, or along the margins of a brushy island or mott. With the advances in GPS technology, land contractors can set out a pattern of islands which provide the correct ratio of open to brushy while perhaps preserving good deer brush or avoiding poorer soils. Take some time to work out any brush program on the maps (soils, aerial, and topographic) and you'll have better results.

On occasion, I consult on places that are old farms or ranches with a good bit of open country. To improve quail utilization of open areas, you need to increase woody cover or at least give the impression of increased woody cover. Brush piles or "teepees" made of old fence posts, if set out in groups of no less than three and no more than 75 yards apart, work pretty well, if the surrounding ground cover is predominantly those "high weeds" I mentioned; weed plants that offer good overhead cover and bare ground underneath, such as broom-weed, doveweed (croton), sunflower, or sesame.

Native forbs (aka weeds, flowers) are best for quail and easy to promote.

New varieties of bundleflower and partridge pea are now on the market that do well in Texas and can be planted in rows, imitating a fencerow; providing good cover as well as excellent food. I also used plain sorghum almum planted in rows the do the same thing. Problem with sorghum almum is it is fairly open at ground level and may be dangerous to livestock should conditions turn dry. A technique developed on the King Ranch involves planting pear cactus in hedgerows and works in very sandy soil. Not to beat a dead horse, but perhaps the best way to increase utilization of old fields remains simple disking in early winter, attempting to bring on the native sunflower. If the project involves an old field, farmed in annual crops in the past, native sunflower is probably in the soil waiting for the stimulus of the disk.

Experience has taught me humility and the need to experiment when making drastic changes in nature. I once designed a reforestation project which involved planting native brush species in a 100 acre field of deep sand. We bought 1,000 brush seedlings from a nursery in the Valley and hired high school students to plant them. We even went so far as to run waterlines to the new "mottes", so the seedlings would get a good start. Of 1,000 seedlings, NONE survived the first year. It turns out that the field was full of rats, living in the grass and cactus, and the rats loved the new seedlings. Point is, if you have plans for a major renovation of anything in Nature, ask around for advice and start on a small scale to see if it really will succeed. The Agricultural Extension Service, the Natural Resource Conservation Service, and the Texas Parks and Wildlife Dept. are great sources for free advice; use them.

Now that you have opened up the brush, leaving at least 20% with woody cover no more than 50 yards in any direction, you have the frame for your quail house. The walls of the house are those herbaceous plants that provide close cover and food for the birds. Good examples are broomweed and croton. Both are dense above, so much so that little grows underneath these plants. Quail feel secure underneath the canopy and can easily find seeds on the bare ground. Native sunflower is another favorite of mine in that it produces a large, oily seed and prohibits growth of other plants beneath it.

Herbaceous cover is nothing more than grass and weeds. As discussed, weeds are the primary food source for quail and are the plants you will see after any soil disturbance. They are the first echelon of succession followed by grasses which are followed by woody plants. We need some grass for nesting cover, but should work to reduce grass cover annually, thereby promoting weeds and further restricting the regrowth of brush. It is a fact of life that neglecting regrowth brush will result in a loss of open country in a very short period of time.

The best way to reduce grass and woody regrowth is by disking. If the area is one of light brush, you can effectively clear it and promote weeds using a rome plow as mentioned in Chapter 2-3. If it is already cleared of woody plants, you can use a farm disk. I like to rotate disked areas, disking annually perhaps 10% of open areas. This can add up over a large ranch, but need not break the budget. For example, on 1,000 acres to be managed for quail, you should have at least 200 acres of brush, leaving 800 acres open. Of the 800 acres, perhaps a fourth is in field or food plots, leaving 600 acres. 10% of that is only 60 acres and you can disk that much in 12 hours with a 12-foot disk. You should try to disk ground that has not been disked in the last three years. This will give you areas of one-year-old disk strips, two-year-old disk strips and the new disked strips. Do your disking in October to March and learn what weeds come up following the disking. In sandy soils in South Texas, native sunflower comes up in fields disked in October-January, while jumbo or three-seeded croton comes up in areas disked after March 15. Adjust these times for climate as I'm sure disking in the Panhandle for weeds would be different than in the Coastal Bend. The point is, you should plan on disking some portion of your cleared areas every year to inhibit grass and woody regrowth and to

Properly timed, light discing will produce forbs for wildlife and reduce grass.

promote weeds. Do NOT disk the same ground more than
once every three years, as that tends to wear the soil out by
depleting the nutrients and the seedbank.

Other techniques for managing vegetation for quail include
burning and grazing. Burning turns back the successional clock
by reducing woody cover, removing dead plants, and returning
nutrients to the soil much quicker than normal decay. It can
speed up sprouting of weeds by reducing competition with
grasses and by warming the soil with solar heat absorbed by
the black ash. Burning is a wonderful tool, but only margin-
ally predictable and quite dangerous. I do not recommend
burning to the novice landowner and strongly advise anyone

not experienced in burning to seek professional guidance. The Natural Resource Conservation Service is an excellent source for assistance and will design and conduct burns on your land for free. Texas Parks and Wildlife is gearing up to do the same and should be able to provide qualified burn masters in the near future.

Grazing, on the other hand, is simple and safe. Problem is, few people understand grazing pressure and plant recovery so most ranches are grazed too close for quail. Removal of all the grass by September means there will not be sufficient nesting cover in the spring. By the time grasses have recovered enough in the spring to provide suitable nesting cover; it is too late in the season for quail chicks to survive the summer heat. You must leave adequate nesting cover in the fall if you want good quail reproduction in the spring. More on grazing in a later chapter, but suffice to say, I do not believe cows and quail can be maximized on the same ground.

It is human nature to want to put out food for wildlife, and most management plans include feeders. Supplementing the food supply with feeders is quick, easy, and gives us a feeling that we are overcoming shortfalls in Nature by sheer force of will. In truth, I do not have much faith in feeders for Bobwhite quail. I've built a good many feeders, put out perhaps hundreds in my life, and certainly filled thousands, but I just don't think they do as much as we think to promote quail survival or reproduction.

The major drawback to feeders for quail as for deer, is that they disrupt normal distribution of the individuals. Because food is readily available and easily consumed, feeders tend to concentrate populations. In the case of deer, this leads to over-browsing in the area of the feeders. In the case of quail, it results in a buffet for predators and a central pick up point for disease. I guess if a feeder was provided for each covey, in good cover, it would be acceptable, but even with that you risk disease from the feed and added predation simply because the predators know when the birds will come to feed. I firmly believe it is far better to work the soil and encourage native food production than to put out feed from a bag. At a minimum, I would limit supplemental feed for quail to broadcasting feed along a road over a large area. I suggest broadcasting the feed to the side, so most of it lands in the brush at a rate of 50 pounds per mile of road, with no more than one-quarter pound per acre applied once a week during the winter months.

Food plots are another quick fix in the minds of many landowners. For quail, this, too, has some drawbacks. First of all, a food plot of sunflower, sorghum or millet only produces food for a short period in the fall. The rest of the time it is either bare ground or growing plants, assuming you receive enough rainfall for a crop at all. Secondly, food plots are limited in the number of coveys they can attract and supplement, simply due to natural dispersion of the coveys. Conversely, disking over the whole management area promotes native plants which are hardier than commercial plants and produce seeds which for the most part are better accepted by the birds and better for them. An acceptable variation is food plots that follow roadways. Planting the margins of roadways provides what food is produced in a more accessible manner and does not disrupt normal foraging routes as much as a plot.

Where existing fields lend themselves to food plots, rather than letting them go back to native vegetation, I prefer to manage them as a rotating food plot. I plant or disk one-third every year, leaving the other two-thirds fallow. I also often combine the seeds for cool season deer plots such as oats with native sunflower or croton, in an attempt to get two crops out of

To reduce loss to aerial predators, adapt your feeder to feed off-road.

one planting. The oats come up in September-October and die off just as the sunflower comes on in March. This can be done in the one-third/two-thirds system mentioned above with good results for deer, quail, and dove. There are other commercially available mixes that try to do the same. Be careful with these mixes as they might not be suitable to your soils or climate.

Also, some commercial seeds require real farming techniques and can be an expensive mistake if not planted properly.

All the research literature on Bobwhite quail and water seems to indicate that quail do not need drinking water at any time in their lives if adequate plant moisture is available. Ignoring that, we went through a period in South Texas where quail waterers were the craze and to this day, you can find small concrete basins on ranches throughout the Rio Grande Plain. I was as guilty as anyone and was instrumental in getting many of those expensive watering basins put in. I believe now that they do not improve quail reproduction or survival and you can benefit from my mistake. However, I do believe there is a place for supplemental water in quail management in a very narrow application. This is just as expensive as watering basins, maybe more so, but thus far seems to be worth it to those who must do all they can to have huntable native birds every year, regardless of the weather.

We have long associated good quail years with good rainfall. The thought was, when it rains, there is abundant food produced, good cover for nesting/brooding, and chick survival is good. That is all true, but one factor that was overlooked was ground temperature. Bobwhite quail chicks are very sensitive to temperature and will perish if they cannot escape the heat. Ground temperature is significantly higher than where our heads are, so a hot day to us is death on the ground for a 2-inch tall quail chick.

Vegetation reduces ground temperature, both by shading the ground and through evaporation of moisture the plant draws from its roots. Leaving adequate ground cover is always a good idea, but may fall short in periods of hot dry weather. I toyed with the idea of supplementing the normal rainfall, using lawn sprinklers set out in the pasture. I put out thermometers, both inside the watered circles and outside, with a thermometer at ground level and at head height. Both thermometers at head height stayed pretty much alike, regardless of the use of the sprinkler, but the two at ground level differed greatly. Inside the watered circle, at ground level, it was consistently 15-18 degrees cooler than outside the watered circle during daylight hours. How would this effect chick survival? Well, say it has been a dry spring and it turns hot early. I believe the hens will continue to hatch chicks, but the lack of insects, critical diet for chicks in the first two weeks, combined with the heat, quickly kills off her brood. If she has a green circle nearby, the chicks can escape the heat and feed on the abundance of insects drawn by the lush, green vegetation.

Problems with this technique include cost of setting out enough sprinklers with sufficient water pressures to make adequate circles, predation on the chicks at a vulnerable time in their life, and manpower to run the system(s). Naturally, if all else is brown, you cannot have cattle around either, and this is sometimes a problem.

As mentioned, this is not for the casual quail manager, and may not improve quail numbers on most ranches. As with buying "improved" genetics for deer management, setting out sprinklers will not correct an overall poor management plan. It does seem to provide some insurance against the weather in some years, and is an example of "tweaking" Mother Nature. In other words, trying to money-whip a problem that may be too big for anyone's budget.

Harvesting quail is somewhat self-limiting; if numbers in the bag go down, so does interest. However, I caution you to guard against over-harvesting your birds if you use feed to draw them to the road. Quail seek to maintain coveys of 12-14 birds, and will reorganize as their numbers drop due to natural causes and hunting. What appears to be a "fresh" covey in late January, may in fact be three partials combined to form one covey. Learn to age quail and use this to determine what your reproductive success was the previous spring. If the percentage of young birds in the bag is high, you can safely harvest more birds. If the ratio of young of the year to mature birds is less than 3 to 1, be careful. As always, try to kill what you shoot at. Providing your guests with the opportunity to shoot some warm up skeet, even if hand-thrown, will help reduce loss to cripples. And use dogs; even a lousy dog is better than you are at finding a cripple and makes the hunt more fun.

Managing Miscellaneous Wildlife

Even the most avid deer hunter, the most fanatic quail hunter, needs something to do in the off season. Miscellaneous wildlife opportunities can extend the seasons and increase your enjoyment of the ranch.

The most common off-season activity is fishing. As discussed, it is important to assess the soil attributes before you buy your ranch. Some soils do not hold water well and some areas may not have enough run-off to maintain a decent-sized impoundment. Assuming you have soils conducive to stocktanks or ponds, and can catch enough rainwater or can supplement a pond with well water, you can easily build and manage surface water facilities for fishing. Design and construction of a pond for fishing is different than for a stocktank. Sure, any hole deep enough to survive the dry spells without getting too warm will sustain fish, but to maximize fishing enjoyment and fish reproduction, certain differences should be included when constructing a fishing pond.

The most important aspect of a fishing pond is bottom contour. You need a pit for those dry/hot spells. Deep water provides a cooler environment for the bigger fish, critical in

July-August. I once hauled 25, 15 pound blocks of ice to a pond that was dying in the heat. Although supplemented by a well, the well had gone down and the pond had drawn down to less than 6 feet, so did not have enough depth. Big bass were rolling belly-up in the pond and the ice bought us time to fix the well. Expensive and perhaps fool-hardy, but it worked. In Medina Co., where I live, the average annual loss to evaporation is 60 inches. Add to that the normal seepage which occurs in even the best clays, and you can see why you need reserve water in a deep pit.

After you have a decent pit, defined as having at least 8 feet of water during even the driest times, you need adjoining pits and trenches connected to the pit. This greatly increases fishing enjoyment and allows the bigger fish to migrate to the pit as water levels go down. Number, size, and location of these secondary pits is limited only by the size of your pond when full as most pond builders charge by the cubic yard moved, regardless of where it is moved, as long as the distances are not extreme. One pond I designed had the main pit along the dam, then five smaller pits radiating out in a star-shaped pattern. The connecting channels should all be as deep as the secondary pits, to prevent trapping fish when the pits go dry.

Within the main pit, you can vary the contour, usually at no extra cost. If the scraper enters and leaves the pit(s) from the same two sides, the remaining two sides will be much steeper, forming drop-offs that hold fish and add to fishing the challenge. Normal preferred slope is a 1:4 to reduce sloughing, but in better clay soil, the slope can be much more severe (steeper) with little danger of sloughing. Bars or fingers can be designed into the main pit to further enhance fishing.

Structure is a catch phrase among fishermen and can be best added before the pond fills. Tires chained together (be sure to drill several holes in the tires to prevent floating), utility poles chained together, discarded farm implements (remove any oil or lubricants), and large trees cleared from the pond site all serve as good structure if properly anchored. New ponds can be fertilized with bales of hay anchored to the sides or bottom or with commercial fertilizer to promote algae growth to start the food chain. Contrary to popular belief, aquatic vegetation is not desired and should be controlled.

Stocking new ponds is usually done in two stages and is fairly inexpensive. Initially, food fish such as fathead minnows and bluegills are stocked to be followed by predator fish, usually Largemouth bass, after the food fish have reproduced. For those in a hurry, larger fish are available for stocking, but cost more and require a larger food supply. Stocking rates depend on the types of fish stocked and the size of the fingerlings. Your fish supplier will recommend the proper stocking rate.

Should you inherit an established lake or pond on your ranch, try to assess the quality of the existing fish population. Older stocktanks will have trash fish, carp and gar, in them, and if that is the case, I recommend killing the tank and re-stocking. If there are quality fish mixed in, it becomes a question of how the trash fish affect the quality of your fishing. Fish the pond several times before you kill it as there is something very final about rotenone.

Feeders are useful in jump-starting a pond and particularly useful if you plan on stocking Channel catfish. I visited one ranch where the feeder was located at the end of a pier. Under the feeder, the landowner had suspended a large basket of chicken wire. Whenever he felt like catfish for dinner, he would wait for the feeder to go off, watch the catfish gather to feed and crank up the basket, full of fish to choose from.

Regardless of the size of your fishing pond, it is very important to properly harvest fish if you want bigger fish. As with high fenced enclosures for deer, a pond must be carefully monitored to maximize growth of the individuals. As a general rule, you should fish the pond frequently, and keep all fish caught. Some landowners use a slot system to preserve a certain class of fishes such as saving all bass under 14 inches. This can backfire on you as soon ALL bass will be less than 14 inches. Conversely, throwing back all fish over 14 inches may eventually result in a large class of mature fish with no forage fish. I believe it is better to keep all fish caught, regardless of size.

Lastly, while on the subject of new ponds, remember to seed the dam (dump) of a new pond. Erosion can quickly gouge a new dam as the soil is not compressed. I recommend planting new dams with a mix of common Bermuda grass and browntop millet. As mentioned earlier, keep trees and brush off the backside of a new dam. You can plant shade trees on the front or water side.

A secondary species gaining a strong following is the wild turkey. Although usually found along waterways, turkey range great distances in the spring for breeding/nesting, and you can draw and hold them on your ranch even if you are some distance from a waterway. Turkeys need mature trees for a roost, high ground vegetation for nesting, and a dependable food supply. If you do not have mature trees, you can build an artificial roost from utility poles and cross timbers. I know of a ranch near the Rio Grande River that is all scrub brush with no trees taller than 15 feet over thousands of acres. They have a good turkey population using the artificial roosts. The vertical posts are all sheathed in metal flashing to prevent nocturnal visits by raccoons/bobcats, and the area is kept isolated. Once you establish a roost or discover one, it is best to leave it alone to avoid spooking the flock.

Turkey feeders work best if off the ground and protected from predators.

Good grazing management is necessary for turkey reproduction, and should be planned well ahead. As with quail, if there are only 10 clumps of grass over an acre of land, predators have an easy time finding the nests and disrupting nesting.

Providing supplemental food for turkeys is easy and rewarding. I use five foot elevated platforms to hold barrels of corn. The platforms would seem to be counter-productive, as they expose turkeys to aerial predators. However, my experience has been that turkeys have little to fear from flying predators, so elevated feed stations work well. The platform can also be sheathed in metal flashing, which prevents raccoons from getting to the feed. I firmly believe that turkeys can smell raccoons; one of their main predators, at a feeder, so keeping them off the platform and away from the feeder reduces stress on the birds and improves utilization.

Feral hogs are a year 'round source of hunting excitement,

even among those landowners who do not encourage them. If your new ranch has feral hogs, and most do, the question will not be one of managing FOR them, but one of controlling their numbers. The best way I know of keeping feral hogs from getting out of hand and disrupting your wildlife management efforts is to deny them access to supplemental feed. Doing so will not eliminate feral hogs, as they have done well in the wild without any help from us, but should keep them from dominating your feeders. This is expensive, as I believe the best way is to enclose all feeders in true hog panels well secured to the ground. An additional factor in the cost is the requirement to make such enclosures large enough to encourage use by deer. A recent study done at A&M Kingsville suggests that such enclosures should be at least 160 feet on a side. While deer will certainly enter an enclosure smaller than that, I believe they should be at least 80 feet on a side for optimum use by deer. The hog panels should be secured with metal "T" posts driven deeply into the ground every five feet and secured with tie wire at two points on each post. Additional benefits seem to derive from making the enclosure a circle instead of a square, which eliminates corners where digging usually occurs.

To reduce feral hog numbers, the occasional hog taken during hunting season is just not enough. Trapping can reduce numbers if done actively all year, and large traps, using pens much like that described above to keep hogs away from feeders, can be very effective. But I believe it is more important to keep the hogs away from supplemental feed and to harvest hogs whenever possible.

Javelina are interesting animals that add romance to any ranch. However, they do not like feral hogs and even with completely different food habits, are rarely found in areas of high feral hog numbers. Keeping feral hog numbers down can help keep javelina on the ranch, as can promoting pear cactus, the primary food item for javelina.

Lastly, dove hunting is very popular across the State and many landowners want to encourage good dove numbers. As Mourning dove are migratory, it is against Federal law to provide supplemental food from a bag to attract dove. However, it is perfectly legal to plant seed-producing crops to attract Mourning doves. I prefer native sunflower fields for Mourning dove, as cattle and deer do not consume native sunflower and thus the fields do not need fencing. Other commercial seed crops such as Peredovic sunflower or milo on the other hand, are attractive to cattle and deer, and should be fenced from cattle at a minimum. As mentioned, simply disking old fields at the right time will bring up native sunflower seed in the soil as well as other native plants attractive to dove such as croton or doveweed. Much of what you do for quail will also benefit any doves passing through.

Managing Livestock

Texas is cattle country, no doubt about it. Our history is replete with legends of great cattle herds and the tough men that moved them. Our landscape over much of the State has been shaped by this history with 24 million acres in the south changed from grassland to brush, more millions out west changed from grassland to desert. This history is in the blood of today's ranch buyer and chances are, you, too, will want to "run cows" on your new ranch. That is fine, even if you bought the ranch primarily for wildlife management, as long as you don't let cattle become the tail wagging the dog.

First of all, your ranch should be under an agricultural valuation for ad valorem taxes, and, after having read the first half of this book, you have ensured that the "exemption" has been transferred to your name. If the ranch had not changed hands in the five years before you bought it, most likely the ag exemption is for cows or farming. Yes, you can change this exemption over to wildlife, but I recommend that new landowners wait awhile for things at the tax office to settle. If the land has been grazed/farmed during the previous five years, you should have a two year grace period before you have to graze, farm, or change the exemption as the law reads "five out of seven". Confirm this with your county appraiser, and then use the time to learn the place and prepare for the arrival of your cows. I'll use cows in this chapter, although you may be just dying to stock sheep, goats, or zebras. My advice throughout this book is based on the tenet held by all field biologists that was first spoken by the great philosopher/ wildlifer, Dale Rollins, "it depends", so it should be general enough to apply to all classes of livestock.

A basic definition of ranching in the modern sense is the confinement of a class or classes of animals in an area so that they will consume the vegetation produced by that area and increase in either quality or numbers so as to produce a profit when the surplus, be it offspring, milk, wool, etc. is sold. Note that the key is the consumption of vegetation *produced by that area*. All ranchers hope that they will not have to supply additional feed to the herd as that comes directly from their profits. To do this successfully, the rancher has to learn how much food is produced by the land and thus how many animals he can run without depleting the food supply. More importantly, to graze it without damaging the recuperative ability of the vegetation. This is a concept we have already discussed, that of carrying capacity.

Carrying capacity is critical to successfully managing a cattle herd and becomes even more critical if you are also managing for wildlife. The wild animals are also dependent on the vegetative production for food as well as cover, and competition with livestock needs to be monitored from several aspects.

Ranching, as with wildlife management, begins with the soil. Different soils produce different vegetation in a given climate. Sandy soil in Bee Co. will produce different plants than clay soils in the same county but sandy soil in Kleberg Co. may produce different plant than that in Bee Co. As mentioned, just as certain soils respond differently to weather they respond differently to grazing pressure. They contain different nutrients and may release those nutrients to the plants differently. Added to this the great variety in rainfall, temperatures, and day length, and it is amazing we can make any long-term plans at all.

Because of this great variety in soils, climate, and livestock classes, it is important that the new landowner seek local advice on carrying capacity. Your best bet would be the county agent, found in the Agricultural Extension Office in each county. In South Texas, I normally start with one Animal Unit (A.U.) per year (AUY) for every 25 acres of native brush. Even within South Texas I fudge this based on where I am, more cows along the coast, less as I move westward. More cows per acre to the north, less as I move southward and of course I adjust with each individual property.

Grazing systems are very important as well. Rather than running 5 animal units (A.U.) continuously on 100 acres with no fences, you might be able to run 10 A.U. on the same 100 acres if you break it into four pastures and rotate the cows through each pasture. This concentrates their grazing while allowing the three non-grazed pastures time to recover. It also favors the improvement of the range, as the cows will graze more evenly as they seek out sustenance during their stay in that pasture. This concept was taken to extremes in the late '70's, early 80's when the Savory or Cell System was the rage. In the cell system, a block of land was divided off into multiple pastures small enough that the herd would consume the entire vegetative surplus in a period of days, and then move onto the next cell. In theory, this maximized grazing efficiency and over time favored the stronger grasses, improving the range. In truth, the systems usually collapsed, simply because we do not have continuous rainfall nor similar temperatures spread throughout the year and at times, grass just doesn't grow.

Random discing breaks up hard pan and promotes water absorption.

Grass grows when it has sunlight, moisture, and suitable temperatures. For most of Texas, these conditions change with the season, and we have two growing seasons, spring and fall. Grass does not grow in the winter as it is too cold, nor does it grow (much) in the summer as it is too hot. If you do not, or cannot in the case of the cell system above, allow for this variation in grass growth, at times your herd will consume more than can be replenished. This is overgrazing, where there are too many animals on an area for the time they are there. They graze off the surplus grass, and then begin destroying the grass plants themselves. When this happens, the soil becomes bare, erosion and hard panning sets in, and you lose overall productivity, sometimes forever. Concurrent with the loss of grazing is the loss of cover and food for wildlife, reducing reproduction and animal vigor.

If wildlife is your primary objective, and if you want to run a permanent herd, you must remain flexible, both in numbers and in grazing management. Landowners become attached to their cows, keeping them long after prudent grazing dictates that some or all be removed. It would be wise to stock light, even in wet years, keeping some of their offspring as a liquid portion of your herd that can be sold if the weather turns against you. For example, say your ranch will run 25 AUY (animal units per year). Rather than stocking it with 25 cows, or 22 cows and two bulls, stock it with 16 cows and two bulls and keep 9 heifers. If it stays wet and grass is good, fine, keep the heifers a year and use them as replacements or sell them. If it turns hot and dry, you have the option of selling them off to preserve the main herd of carefully culled mama cows and protecting your range.

Perhaps a better option is to use steers, either your own or a leaseholders to reduce grass on your ranch. Steers are valued at .7 of an A.U., and since they are only on the ranch for 6 months, you can almost double the total A.U. For example, if your ranch will run 25 A.U.Y., then it would run almost 38 steers or heifers. Since they will only be there for half of the year, you can double that number to 76. A word of caution here, since steers are not "gentled" as are mature cows, running steers requires good fencing and good pens. I have been present on two occasions when a truckload of steers, released on a new ranch, left the ranch completely before stopping for air. Receive them in good pens; let them settle for a few hours, and then provide feed and water. After a couple of days, ease them out to pasture.

Steers more closely resemble the buffalo in their impact on rangeland. Buffalo used to roam freely, eating everything to the ground, then moving on to greener pastures. Because of this, I believe steers are better for use in a wildlife management plan than are cows. Current research seems indicate that more grass is better, certainly for quail if not for all species. Using

Having an irrigated field is an asset in livestock management.

steers allows the landowner the flexibility of NOT grazing
every year if conditions are not right and it may well be that
conditions are right for grazing only every other year or every
third year. This, too, is a great plus in the use of wildlife as the
basis for your ag exemption. You don't have to graze, but you
can when you need to, and you should. I fear some ranches
under agricultural valuation for wildlife have become rank
with old grass; reducing forb growth and impeding traffic of
quail. Grazing, burning, or discing are often applied as an
"emergency" fix, never a good idea.

Since fields produce more grass than rangeland, it is normal
for ranchers to want to put in fields. As I mentioned earlier,

you will probably inherit some fields when you buy your ranch. If the fields are properly fenced and watered, and in good soils, you can manage them for your cows. Having a field that can support the herd for an extended period of time gives your range time to recover and you time to decide what you're going to do if things go south.

Lastly, on the subject of grazing, placing supplements at the far reaches of each pasture will help grazing distribution. Cows will go a long way for salt and it is counterproductive to place the salt next to water. They drink, lick some salt, and then go only as far as they have to the graze, often leaving the area around water sources a barren desert.

Equally important as grass, it is imperative that cows have access to dependable sources of water. It needn't be the sweetest, cleanest, coolest water in Texas, but it better be dependable or you've got problems. I was told that a mature cow in the heat of summer consumes 16 gallons of water a day. That is more than three minutes of top production for most windmills, so unless your new ranch has riverfront, you should plan for reserves.

Going back to the ranch I developed in Charlotte, we had earthen tanks, but they were old and had no pits, so were not dependable. We had one good well with a 5 hp. electric submersible that put out 40 g.p.m., but had no reservoir. On 1,600 acres, we planned to stock at a rate of 1 A.U. per 20 acres (we had some field), so needed water for 80 A.U. The ranch was some distance from town, and I knew when I needed a well guy, everyone else would too, so I figured on at least five days of reserves: 80 X 16 X 5 = 6,400 gallons. We put in an 8,000 gallon concrete reservoir and piped it to a central lane then to all pastures and never had a problem.

Distribution of water is important and systems can be installed now that make it cheaper to pipe water to distant troughs than to dig a well there. Existing waterlines can be adapted to serve wildlife uses as we have discussed, and can be used to improve both wildlife and livestock distribution. Cattle should never have to travel more than one mile to water; anything more and they will not properly utilize the whole pasture. Consider water when you design your pastures. Almost all the ranches I've consulted on could improve their grazing efficiency by simply moving fences. Try to set up your fencing so that the pastures are equally productive, not equal in size. On the other hand, if your ranch is already well fenced and cross-fenced, evaluate each pasture as to carrying capacity and improve those that are less productive. Pasture A should be able to support as many cows as Pasture B, C, or D for the same period of time. Clearing brush will increase forage productivity and can be worked into your brush program for wildlife.

The normal annual schedule for cows goes something like this: Calves are born in Jan., Feb., and March, wormed, castrated, and tagged in April, and sold at weaning sometime in September. Bulls should only be with the cows during April, May, and June to produce calves when the grass is greening up just as they come off of milk. How does this schedule affect wildlife? Well, for deer, as long as the cows have enough to eat and are not forced to eat browse, and there is enough ground cover to hide new fawns from predators, there is not much conflict. Calves are gone during hunting season, so it is just the mama cows and the bulls. Deer hunters piss and moan about cows being around when they are hunting, but deer really don't mind them and you'll often see them together on an oats patch. Quail and turkey are much more sensitive to grazing pressure as I've mentioned, with regards to both food and cover. In addition, if grazing is limited, cows can destroy nests, either by trampling or by exposing the eggs to sunlight and predation. Cows can affect all wildlife by removing vegetation from around watering sources, making it much more difficult to access water safe from predators.

As long as cows are carefully controlled, removed as soon as they begin to impact on wildlife reserves of vegetation for both food and cover, and the landowner knows to plan ahead for future wildlife needs, they can be a valuable tool and add to the total enjoyment of the ranch. Needless to say, if the landowner needs to maximize income from cows, chances are wildlife will suffer.

TIMING YOUR PURCHASE
AND IMPROVEMENTS

Does it make any difference when you buy your ranch, when you high fence a ranch, when you dig a new stocktank? In this section, I provide some suggestions as to when to implement your plans, either for buying or developing your new ranch.

When to Buy

Below are my sales for the last several years. I deal in ranches from 500 acres to 5,000, and work with buyers who primarily want their ranch for wildlife enjoyment, with or without extensive management. The buyers come from all walks of life; some pay cash, some use financing, all variations with wildlife as the common thread. I only have one buyer currently who is looking for land for cattle ranching. At today's prices, I believe he will be looking for a LONG time!

JAN	FEB	MAR	APR	MAY	JUN
1	3	3	1	1	5

JUL	AUG	SEP	OCT	NOV	DEC
2	2	5	3	2	1

As you can see, most of my closings occur in June thru September with very few closings in the winter months. This means we started looking right after hunting season and that is the busiest time for ranch Brokers. Hunting season is over and people who were hunting on leased land are fed up with their landlord or the quality of wildlife on their lease, and want to get their own place. This is also when most ranches come on the market because landowners wanted to hunt the ranch one last time, or had leases to honor. After the season is over, they want to get it sold before everything turns brown in the summer heat.

As a buyer, you can use this knowledge to your advantage by doing your homework during the hunting season. Admittedly, most ranches will not be officially listed and thus unavailable for showings. But some leftovers from the last year will be available to see. Even with hunters going in and out, you can look at ranches and practice learning a ranch. Types of brush, water systems, improvements, etc. can be learned during the winter, even if the ranch you're looking at does not suit you. It is good to see these places in the winter as well. Grasses are dormant and you can see the effects of over-grazing best in late winter. Wildlife is being harvested and there are always new pictures of deer to teach you about genetics and management results. Landowners are touchy about showings during the season, but will usually work around the hunters. If you run into someone not happy with you and your Broker being there, be graceful and leave; they have guns. I showed a place in Zavala Co. one afternoon and as we drove past the HQ, I waved at a hunter. Later, I noticed him following us and I stopped to visit. He was quite angry with me as he did not know the ranch was for sale and blamed it on me. Needless to say, we moved out smartly and called before we returned.

Once you get into the "rush" period after hunting season, look at any ranch that interests you as soon as you can. Depending on the economy and oil prices, it may be a Seller's market and I have seen numerous ranches sell before I could even get a decent package to my Buyer. It is not unlike a feeding frenzy with the choicest morsels going to the quickest shark. That is not to say you should choose rashly. If you have had the time to study the area, know what you want and where, you can move quickly when the right place comes along. With that in mind, it is good to have your financing lined up before you start looking. I hate to get in a bidding war with another broker and his buyer only to hear my buyer ask where he could get good financing. Someone already qualified has the upper hand in negotiations over one that does not.

Another reason it is good to buy during early in the summer it that it allows you time to plan what you want to do and get some of the work done before hunting season. C'mon, you bought the ranch to enjoy, leave time to go hunting and relax. It never hurts, either, to get the previous owner's cattle off the ranch before September. Even with previous heavy grazing, September rains will give you some grass and weeds for next springs' nesting.

Another active period in ranch sales is just before hunting season. Sellers are panicky if they need or want to sell before the season, and you can get some deals. Sometimes you may have to honor a hunting lease for one of these deals, but it may be worth it to get a good price. The feeding frenzy is over and the picking might appear slim, but work with your broker, the NRCS, and your brush contractor to see if a sows' ear bought cheaply could be turned into a silk purse for a reasonable sum.

Lastly, if you've looked all spring and summer and not found your ranch, consider buying for resale. Look at buying a smaller place or one without the house you want and spending the winter fixing it up for the next frenzy. You'll gain experience and have something that will sell quickly, maybe making you a little money in the bargain.

Timing Your Improvements

Every new landowner wants to get started right away with his plan; tearing up brush, building his house, digging that new lake. Regardless of when you close, take time to schedule your improvements and you'll not only save time, you'll get better results. A review of the most common ranch improvements and the best time to implement them follows. Of course, I realize all work is dependent on the budget, so some things may have to wait a year or two, but hopefully you saved a small pile to get things rolling. I sold a place to a guy one time and he and I had plans for major improvements to the ranch. Just then, a neighbor walked up and asked if he wanted to buy his place at the same price. As the neighbors place was a good bit better, my client jumped at it. Now he owned twice as much land, but had nothing for improvements. Even though it meant hunting out of ground blinds for a year, and camping out in an old shack, I think it was a wise move then and do now. While it may take him three or four years to make all his planned improvements, he'll have a better ranch for it.

Good fences make for good neighbors.

High fencing may be hard to schedule simply because it is such a growth industry. Quality fence builders have the upper hand and until recently were booked months in advance. However, the decline in oil prices have slowed fencing down a bit and some have had to go out of business. From a management standpoint, it is better to high fence before hunting season, so you can begin culling right away. If you cannot start that soon, you can still make some progress by culling inferior bucks and thinning out the doe segment of the herd. Always work on feral hogs, and if you put up feeders, be sure to budget for pens. There's no reason to attract a lot of hogs THEN put up a high fence.

If your ranch adjoins good habitat, and there is no indication of excessive hunting over the fence, consider leaving it low-fenced. Unless you simply have to have all four sides fenced, maybe you can get by with only two or three sides high fenced. You could be fencing out a cooperative neighbor that would favor joining in with you in a management plan that would benefit you both.

Rootplowing should be done either in late winter or mid-summer so the new ground can be planted with some chance of success. If you try to plant new ground in late spring it burns up, and in late fall, you are limited to oats or rye that only have to be replaced with something else in the spring. An exception would be old field. That should be cleared in late fall/ early winter if you think you can get a response from native sunflower. Look for old sunflower stalks to help you decide if the seed is present in the soil.

If the brush work is extensive, with an estimated time of completion of more than one month, you can really start at any time. Mechanical failures and rainy days will extend the job and with that much land cleared, you'll need to plant as they go along. Most contractors will throw out something behind the tractor, either sorghum almum in the warmer months or oats in the cooler months, to reduce loss to erosion. I prefer browntop millet to sorghum almum, as mentioned, because is seeds out quicker and is still cheap. An alternative to having it thrown out by the operator is having it flown on. Any cheap seed will do, as your objective is to hold the soil until you get it all done then you can plant the more expensive seed. If you plan to use a mulcher, rome disk, or roller-chopper, to clear brush timing is not as important as native forbs/grasses will recover.

Pond construction is best done in mid to late summer. July

and August have the least average rainfall and thus present the best chance of getting the hole dug without filling prematurely. I have plans for a 35 acre lake that were written in October. The contractor is on hold, waiting for August when we hope to get it done in two weeks of hopefully dry weather. Conversely, another client tried to enlarge a lake all winter long. Either it was too muddy from foggy drizzle for the equipment to effectively move the heavy clay, or we would get a brief rain and the damn thing would catch a foot or two of water, necessitating a delay while they drained it out to dry. At least we know the lake is in a good location.

Planting commercial warm season seeds should be done when the soil temperature reaches 55 degrees. South of San Antonio, that usually occurs around March 15. This of course varies with location, so ask around and the locals will know when to plant. Cool season seeds should go in the ground in late September to early October. Some people wait until they have a good rain before planting. I prefer to "dust them in" and have the seed waiting in the ground for that rainfall. Whenever you plant anything, take time to do it as best as you can; the effort will pay off.

Water system work should be done in winter. The well service people are looking for something to do and if you have to be without water for an extended period of time, it's no big deal.

New housing, new barns, and new power, should be started as soon as you own the place. It is a sorry fact that construction of any kind in rural areas is expensive and often troublesome. You need someplace to store your equipment and rest your weary body that is out of the weather and comfortable. All things being equal, I'd start on creature comforts first.

Always nice to have a hot shower and shady porch when the day is done.

Managing the Smaller Ranch

While it is a fact that most of us Texans or Texas-transplants cannot own a 10,000 acre spread, or a 1,000 acres for that matter, does not mean we cannot manage and enjoy what piece of this great State we are lucky enough to own. Whether you own 30 acres or 300, there are still things you can do to enhance productivity on your land. Smaller tracts easily make up 99% of Texas ranches and it is to those buyers/landowners that I direct this chapter.

Concerns you have as a small tract owner include neighbors of course, and habitat limitations, both size and diversity. Neighbors are always a major concern when assessing any property for purchase. Buying a ranch with bad neighbors is like marrying a slacker. Don't buy the ranch thinking you can change the neighbors or "live with them"; their shortcoming will just grate over time and detract from your enjoyment of the new ranch, even more so if your ranch is small enough to hear them no matter where you are on your own place. If your primary reason for buying a ranch is deer hunting, you do not want to be in a subdivision of 5 acre or even 25 acre tracts. Sorry, regardless of what the salesman might say, hunting simply will not be "great" in this situation. For the true "ranch hunting" experience, whatever the species, you need to find the dream ranch, which I define as at least 100 acres adjoining a larger place with a low common fence. You can live with one small neighbor, but not three and certainly not four. One small neighbor can be high fenced out if over-hunting is a problem, two at the most. For deer hunters, high-fencing three sides or four makes you a deer pen, not the most enjoyable sport hunting scenario. It may take a bit longer and you may have to go a bit further afield to find a small tract with larger neighbors, but it can be done. Remember, too, if you become the "bad neighbor", the larger ranch will eventually high fence you out, then you're an outcast and your property has lost value. Work at being a good neighbor and don't give them a reason to fence you out.

If your primary purpose for buying a ranch is to hunt deer, work to make your tract both inviting and secure. Make the center of the property a sanctuary for deer, avoiding traffic in the center, leaving the brush undisturbed, and add a bulk feeder; perhaps water if it's reasonable. I prefer the Stand and Fill from Texas Hunter or the Lamco tray feeder because both are low-maintenance. That's not to say a 300 acre block of guajillo is an ideal situation, as even guajillo is unpalatable at times and deer need forbs as part of a normal diet. Judicious clearing and/ or manipulation of fields can provide these forbs, improving available native foodstuffs and better holding the deer in place. No matter what you do, short of high fencing, remember that normal range for a doe is 300 acres, for a breeding buck, it can be 3,000 acres, so best case is a large neighbor that does not mind "sharing" deer, and/or a wildlife management co-op. Such a co-op, made up of like-minded neighbors is a way for smaller landowners to manage for a common good. Texas Parks & Wildlife actively seeks to form these co-ops and will assist in forming the group and managing the assets.

If your primary purpose in buying a place is to fish, or hunt other species such as quail, hogs, or a migratory species; dove, duck, etc., then size is not as important. I bought my place for quail and while it certainly has limitations, if properly situated and managed, I believe you can have huntable quail on less than 500 acres. Turkey are travelers, so you may have problems on a small tract with bad neighbors, but if you can own the roost, you're all set. Otherwise place a feeder or two on platforms, keep them filled and varmint-free and you should have the flock at least travel across your place. Dove, duck, and fish of course require dependable water. In South Texas, this means a pond of at least one acre with a minimum of 8 feet of dependable water year 'round. This requirement can be easily met on 50 acres assuming a good watershed (or a big water well), and good water-retention soils. For duck, I like to have a sizeable portion of the pond extend over shallow flats that can be farmed for small grains then flooded. This requires a supplemental water source or timely rains. Dove do best with a margin of bare ground around the water source. If supplemented, fill the pond full in July and late Nature lower the level for you. If not, bring in cows mid-Summer and you'll have your bare ground margin. Quail are more sensitive to habit manipulation and have fairly precise requirements. I discuss these in detail a bit later.

Your habitat requirements for all species in general, are simple; you need diversity. Some old field, some light brush, some heavier brush/trees, and accessible, dependable water. You need diversity to ensure a variety of foods are available throughout the year and because animals live on the "edge", literally. Wild animals like to be close to good escape cover

Discing in old field and along roadways increases diversity.

and will utilize your smaller tract more completely if you have a diversity of cover. Whatever you do, if management of any non-migratory wildlife species is important to you, do not manicure your property. Sure, mow the grass around the camp and a portion around the ponds, but leave it natural and keep the vegetation in turmoil by discing/burning/grazing periodically. A "rough" looking ranch is a productive ranch whereas a tidy ranch may be sterile. Specific percentages of cover/food vegetation types vary with species and should be researched individually. Excellent literature is available online both from TP&W as well as the Agrilife Extension Service.

With regards to "but what should I do on my place?", rather than speak in hypotheticals, I believe I'll just tell you what I did on my own small place and how I manage it. Certainly, what I do does not apply to every ranch, but my experiences on my little tract should at least point out areas where you need to ask questions.

I have been blessed with 124 acres in Medina Co. and think it may be a perfect size for me as I can walk the place in a couple of hours, but still find new aspects each time I go out. I manage for quail primarily, but have dove, deer, and turkey in huntable numbers as well. Management is for recreational hunting and wildlife observation by family and friends.

My soil is primarily a clay loam, not the sand I would have preferred, but it is only 3.5 miles from my home, so I accepted the trade-off. A plus of the soils is they all hold water well, so the ponds are fairly dependable. The land was in field 20 years ago and has some good-sized mesquite/Huisache regrowth. It was fenced into three pastures of 30, 30, and 65 acres, so I split the bigger one for a four pasture rotation. I purchased the place and added "city" water although it has three good ponds on it. With the new pasture configuration, I need city water in two of the four pastures. It adjoins a rural subdivision, so city water was readily available. If that had not been the case, I would have drilled a well. I paid a pretty penny for power, and built a small shop/cabin on it. As mentioned, I manage primarily for quail/dove, although I welcome any wildlife that stumbles onto the place.

Bobwhite quail have a home range that varies with quality. An accepted management goal is one bird to the acre, so on 124 acres of perfect habitat, I could have 124 birds or about 8.8 coveys. If I "steal" birds from the neighbors who do not hunt, I can increase my population somewhat, so I broadcast feed along the perimeter starting in September. Additionally, I leave fence lines brushy, manage grazing so I always have not only adequate nesting cover, but good ground cover to reduce temperatures, and I do a lot of half-cutting to increase woody cover close to the ground. From the truck it looks wooded, but if you get down to a quail's level, it is just trunks and grass.

Half-cutting, combined with grazing and discing, increases cover at their level as well as food. This is important to increase usable space in old fields. Because it was once all field, and planted in coastal Bermuda, I must have cows to reduce the grass cover and promote weeds. I split the big pasture because I want the cows to be focused on a relatively small area so they will uniformly graze all species of grass, but really hammer the Bermuda. Cows are stocked at a rate of 1 AU to 20 acres and only on the place for 90-120 days starting when quail nesting starts in late April. Assuming they have adequately grazed the Bermuda down, they leave in August which hopefully gives the grass time to recover enough to provide nesting cover for the next year. If they have not removed enough grass, I let them stay a bit longer, but nesting cover is critical to quail. I'd rather increase stocking for the 90 days than have them on for 120.

I shred random strips through the brush and disk those strips lightly in winter to encourage weeds. There is one spot near the larger pond that is fairly flat and devoid of regrowth. I plan to manage this 5 acres or so for native sunflower. Native sunflower is present on the place, and I think if I disk this patch in Dec.-Jan. I will get a decent stand. If that works, there are other spots that I can try.

Deer are a secondary management objective, and, as the property is low-fenced on three sides and too open for deer to "live" on the place, I installed a deer blind and two feeders near the center of the ranch for friends to hunt, (hint: never put a blind or feeder on the boundary). This works and we see deer even in my lighter brush. You can tell by the trails from neighboring, more heavily wooded neighbors where we are recruiting "our" deer from. I fill the feeders in a 1:5 milo to corn mix to further supplement quail, anchoring a covey or two, although my primary method for supplementing quail is broadcasting the milo off-road. I feel it is important to feed off-road to reduce exposure to predators. After years of adapting feeders, Texas Hunter has come up with an offset for bumper receivers that has just the right angle. In truth, food is rarely limiting in wild quail populations but I do it mostly because it increases my chances of seeing the little guys.

Turkey are plentiful through no action on my part, and I have installed a feeder on a platform just to keep them close to the house for viewing. The largest of the three ponds could hold fish, but needs cleaning out. Problem is, it has never gone dry enough for equipment to work it. Traditionally, in an instance like this, you would go below the old dam and dig a new pond. However, proximity to the boundary precludes this in my case, so I'll have to wait until it gets dry enough for a track-loader to work the edges. Being a clay soil, it would take a full year of no added water for it to get dry enough for a 'dozer or scraper to get in there.

So, in a nutshell, that's what I've done on my 124 acres. Certainly not the Ponderosa, but it suits my needs and has proven to be very productive. Depending on what you want your ranch to do, buying right and managing intelligently can be very rewarding and lots of fun.

Section 4

CONCLUSION

Giving advice on anything is tricky and giving advice on something as significant as the purchase of a ranch can be downright suicidal. As this is the second edition of the book, I have responded to gripes about the first try and hope I have addressed most of them. I know this book does not cover East Texas, West Texas, the Panhandle, or that sweet 200 acres you've been looking at outside of Waco, but in a sense, it really does. Finding a broker to represent you rather than relying on the broker representing the seller is always important no matter where you're looking. Learning where you want to be, researching soils and rainfall, learning some important plants on sight, these are universal as well. And spending a little extra to have your own attorney review the contract and the minerals is just good common sense.

I freely admit that the wildlife management advice is straight from South Texas, maybe a bit into Central Texas, but that's where I've been all my professional life. I can only write what I know about and ask that you bear with me and do a little homework on your own. This book does not address every aspect of every acre in the state, but that is the beauty of owning land in Texas. Each and every one of the 172,044,800 acres in this beautiful state are unique and the process of buying some for you and your family can be both daunting as well as rewarding. I hope my 25 years' experience helping buyers assess ranch property, then getting their dream ranch bought will prove helpful. But do not limit yourself to this small book. Since the first edition there has been an explosion of information on the process of ranch acquisition and management. Do some research, have fun, and get you a piece of that heaven we call Texas.

Locking your gate for the first time is a great feeling.

Online Resources and Recommended Reading

1. SOURCES FOR REAL ESTATE

- The Livestock Weekly: www.livestockweekly.com
- The Houston Chronicle: www.chron.com
- The San Antonio Express-News: www.mysanantonio.com
- The Corpus Christi Caller-Times: www.caller.com
- Lands of Texas: www.landsoftexas.com
- Texas Farm and Ranch Magazine: www.farmandranch.com
- Texas Land Brokers Association: www.texaslandbrokers.com
- Farm and Ranch Marketplace: www.farmranchproperty.com
- The Real Estate Center, Texas A&M University: www.recenter.tamu.edu
- The Texas Real Estate Commission: www.trec.state.tx.us
- Texas Association of Realtors: www.texasrealtors.com

2. SOURCES FOR DEVELOPMENT/MANAGEMENT

- Texas Cooperative Extension Service: www.texnat.tamu.edu
- Texas Parks and Wildlife: www.tpwd.state.tx.us
- Caesar Kleberg Wildlife Research Institute: www.ckwri.tamuk.edu

- Natural Resources Conservation Service: www.nrcs.usda.gov
- Maptech Mapping Software: www.maptech.com
- Texas A&M Wildlife Department: www.wildlife.tamu.edu
- The Center for Grazinglands and Ranch Mgmt: www.cnrit.tamu.edu/cgrm

3. **MISCELLANEOUS SITES**
   - Texas Wildlife Association: www.texas-wildlife.org
   - The Weather Channel: www.weather.com
   - Texas and Southwestern Cattle Raisers Association: www.texascattleraisers.org

4. **RECOMMENDED READING/REFERENCE**
   - Wildflowers of Texas, by Geyata Ajilvsgi, Shearer Pub.
   - Tree, Shrubs, & Cacti of South Texas, by Everitt & Drawe, Texas Tech University Press
   - A Field Guide to Common South Texas Shrubs, by Taylor, Rutledge, and Herrera, Texas Parks & Wildlife, Pub.
   - Field Guide to the Broad-leaved Herbaceous Plants of South Texas, by Everitt, Drawe, and Lonard, Texas Tech University Press
   - Texas Range Plants, by Hatch and Pluhar, Texas A&M University Press
   - Farm Management, Second Edition, by Ronald Kay, McGraw-Hill
   - Brush Management: Past, Present, and Future, by Wayne Hamilton, A&M University Press
   - Producing Quality Whitetails, by Al Brothers and Murphy Ray, Texas Wildlife Association.
   - Beef, Brush, and Bobwhites, by Dr. Fred Guthery
   - Assorted pamphlets available from Texas Cooperative Extension Service, Natural Resources Conservation Service, and Texas Parks and Wildlife. Most are free and available for the asking.

www.ingramcontent.com/pod-product-compliance
Lightning Source LLC
Chambersburg PA
CBHW051521170526
45165CB00002B/555